An Introduction to
Twentieth-Century Italian Literature

NEW READINGS
Introductions to European Literature and Culture
Series editor: Nicholas Hammond

An Introduction to Twentieth-Century Italian Literature

A Difficult Modernity

Robert S.C. Gordon

Duckworth

First published in 2005 by
Gerald Duckworth & Co. Ltd.
90-93 Cowcross Street, London EC1M 6BF
Tel: 020 7490 7300
Fax: 020 7490 0080
inquiries@duckworth-publishers.co.uk
www.ducknet.co.uk

A catalogue record for this book is available
from the British Library

ISBN 0 7156 3437 2

Typeset by Ray Davies
Printed and bound in Great Britain by
Biddles Ltd, King's Lynn, Norfolk

Contents

Preface

Literature interacts in complicated ways with the movements of history that surround it. On the one hand, there is no easy formula which dictates that literature is always directly shaped by the socio-economic infrastructure in the world or by dramatic events in history. On the other hand, literature cannot be said to exist as a sealed-off system, out on its own, in dialogue only with itself. Somewhere between these two extremes lies a more nuanced relationship between literature and history, in which the evolution of literature when taken over an extended period of time (a century, say) can be read as symptomatic and illuminating of the underlying threads of historical change in the world around it. Looked at in this 'symptomatic' way, literary history becomes less about compiling a series of pigeon-holes for authors, *oeuvres*, movements and dates, and more about teasing out the multiple connections between texts and patterns of context.

Italy in the twentieth century offers a compelling opportunity to study this mediated bond between literature and history. The reason for this is hinted at in the subtitle of this book. In one way or another, both the literature and the broader history of this period in Italy was dominated by one overarching and often fraught struggle: to come to terms with 'modernity', with the various exhilarating and appalling 'shocks of the new' that the twentieth century brought with it.

The history of 'modern' Italy begins, of course, not with the twentieth century, but with the extraordinary story of its unification into a modern nation-state ('The Risorgimento'), a process which

stretched from the late eighteenth century until the declaration of
the Italian nation in 1861, and on into the difficult early years of
nation-building. But if the nineteenth century was politically tu-
multuous for Italy, it also proved economically, socially and
culturally stagnant compared to many of its European neighbours,
leaving a fragile legacy to the new century. Only in the very final
years of the nineteenth century (long after the spread of the industrial revolution in Northern Europe, for example) did Italy begin to
see concrete signs of economic and social modernisation, in the
form of industrialisation (in the North of the country at least),
urbanisation and the politicisation of the working class. The late
nineteenth century also saw the arrival, in Italy as elsewhere, of a
series of key symbols of modernity, such as the telegraph and the
telephone, the cinema and the automobile. Modernisation continued in fits and starts in the following decades under liberal, Fascist
and then republican governments, entering a second particularly
intense phase in the late 1950s and early 1960s, a period that came
to be known as the 'economic miracle' or the 'boom'. This period
saw not only further industrialisation but also Italy's plunge into
that other form of modern economy and culture, consumerism, fed
by the ever-more present mass medium of television (launched in
1954). So it is no exaggeration to say that the twentieth century in
Italy coincided almost exactly with a phase of rapid and variously
convulsive and recalcitrant modernisation.

To say that this entry into 'modernity' was 'difficult', as the
subtitle of this book suggests, would be something of an under-
statement, given that it was a partial cause of bouts of civic unrest
(1890s; 1919-20), two World Wars (1915-1918; 1940-45), the second culminating in occupation and civil war, a twenty-year Fascist
dictatorship in between (1922-43/5), terrorism (1969-1980), and
the near-dissolution of the traditional, agrarian social patterns and
economies that had dominated the history of the Italian peninsula
for millennia. Furthermore, the latter brought with it a massive
displacement of millions of Italians from the country to the cities,
and indeed to other countries and continents altogether. Moder-

nity also, of course, brought great leaps of progress, for example in the form of the enfranchisement of ordinary men (and women too, after the Second World War), the installation of republican democracy, mass education and literacy, improved health and a great deal of prosperity.

As we will see throughout this book, the voices of literary culture, the writers and intellectuals, responded to these and many other transformations with an often bewildering combination of anxiety, resistance and enthusiasm which reflected many of the contradictions and difficulties inherent in the processes of modernisation itself. Their response was particularly charged and intense because, as the century progressed, it became more and more clear that the very idea of 'culture' itself was being transformed. By the end of the twentieth century, literature and the arts, in their forms and the spaces allotted to them, were almost unrecognisable when compared to a century earlier, occupying a strange niche in one corner of a sprawling, hugely varied world of mass culture, stretching from the internet to television and cinema to print media, often only loosely bound to any single country, language or medium. Of course, literature had always belonged in a niche, mostly the preserve of a tiny, educated élite: the difference now was not so much in terms of diminished quantity (if anything, *more* people had access to, time for, and the educational tools to absorb literature than at any time in the past), but in terms of the growth around traditional cultural forms of other, ubiquitous channels for expressing imagination and reflection, pleasures, fantasies and desires; in other words, what used to be the privileged preserve of the artist. The seepage between the two ends of the spectrum – 'high' culture and 'mass' culture – was one of the persistent themes of the century.

The tensions that recurred again and again within the literature of the period, between the impulse for renewal and the impulse for resistance to the new, energised and propelled a century of extraordinary literary creativity. As suggested above, rather than treating a canon of major texts and major authors one by one, in a steady chronology, hoping to cover the field in a comprehensive fashion, this book prefers to look for illuminating paths through the labyrinth of the century's literature in a series of key motifs of modernity (and of reactions against it). In picking this particular perspective on the twentieth century, the book undoubtedly privileges certain figures and moments over others: so, for example, the Futurists, in the early part of the century, and the work of Italo Calvino from the second half of the century will both recur with some frequency in what follows, since in their very different ways both were consistently and explicitly fascinated with modernity and made every effort to reshape literature in reaction to it. Similarly, whereas most chapters and sections will range over a number of texts and authors, certain chapters or sections of chapters will focus on single writers or works, for reasons of significance and influence, or simply because they illustrate the motif or issue in question in an exemplary fashion. So, Luigi Pirandello, Italo Svevo, Eugenio Montale and Primo Levi dominate Chapter 7; and Carlo Emilio Gadda is a guiding presence in the discussion of experimental writing in Chapter 8. Throughout, we will be interested at one and the same time in the general phenomena of modernity, common to the richer modern nations and, on occasion, to large parts of the rest of the world also; in the local Italian inflections given to those international phenomena; and also in specific aspects of Italy's modern history which mark it as in some way peculiar or exceptional in its responses to modernity.

Chapters 1 and 2 lay out certain crucial foundations for an analysis of this kind, such as the questions of national identity and language, the spaces and institutions of literature, and the dogged persistence of a sense of tradition as the perceived vocation of high culture. Chapters 3 to 8 then trace some of the key motifs of modernity within literature, from the cities, machines and migrations of the modern world (Chapter 3) to modern warfare (Chapter 4), from our modern sense of self as defined both in the public sphere (Chapter 5) and in the private sphere of identity (Chapter 6), to the fragmentation of both self (Chapter 7) and traditional literary form (Chapter 8).

An outline chronology of the century is included at the start for orientation. Each chapter is followed by suggestions for further reading (mostly in English) and a glossary of the major authors of the century is provided at the end of the book. Titles of works are given in the original Italian with English translation at their first mention, and then in Italian only after that. All translations from Italian are mine.

Acknowledgements

My thanks are due to any number of teachers, students and colleagues in the twenty years or so since I first began learning about modern Italian literature. I would like to express my particular gratitude to Nick Hammond, first for inviting me to contribute to the New Readings series and then for his encouragement, patience and advice in the ensuing years; to Deborah Blake at Duckworth; to Guido Bonsaver; to Peter Hainsworth and Pierpaolo Antonello, for reading and helping me improve on earlier drafts of the book; and to Barbara Placido, who made it possible for me to complete the book while immobilised with a broken leg. The book is dedicated to Beniamino Gordon, who gave me ample opportunity to think about literature and other things in middle of the night.

Chronology

Year	Italian literature	Italian history
1900		Assassination of Umberto I
1903		Giovanni Giolitti's first government
1904	Luigi Pirandello, *Il fu Mattia Pascal*	
1906	Sibilla Aleramo, *Una donna*	
1909	Filippo Tomaso Marinetti, 'Fondazione e manifesto del futurismo'	
1911	Guido Gozzano, *I colloqui* Aldo Palazzechi, *Il codice di Perelà*	Libyan War (1911-12)
1912	Scipio Slataper, *Il mio Carso*	Males over 25 given vote
1913	Carlo Michelstaedter, *La persuasione e la rettorica* Grazia Deledda, *Canne al vento*	
1914	Dino Campana, *Canti orfici*	Great War (Italy neutral) Interventionist movement
1915		Italy declares war on Austro-Hungary and Germany
1916	Luigi Chiarelli, *La maschera e il volto*	
1917	Pirandello, *Così è (se vi pare)*	Defeat at Caporetto
1918		Victory over Austrians
1919	Federgio Tozzi, *Con gli occhi chiusi*	Versailles Peace Conference D'Annunzio's occupation of Fiume (1919-20) Foundation of Fascist movement 'Biennio rosso' (1919-20): wave of strikes
1921	Giuseppe Antonio Borgese, *Rubè* Pirandello, *Sei personaggi in cerca d'autore*	Foundation of PCI ('Partito comunista italiano')
1922	Pirandello, *Enrico IV*	March on Rome (28 Oct) Mussolini takes power
1923	Italo Svevo, *La coscienza di Zeno*	

Year	Italian literature	Italian history
1924	Achille Campanile, *Tragedie in due battute*	Murder of Matteotti
1925	Eugenio Montale, *Ossi di seppia*	
1926	Pirandello, *Uno, nessuno e centomila*	Opposition banned
1928		Gramsci sentenced to 20 years
1929	Alberto Moravia, *Gli indifferenti*	Lateran Pacts between Italy and Vatican
1930	Corrado Alvaro, *Gente in Aspromonte*	
1931	Giuseppe Ungaretti, *L'allegria*	
1932	Salvatore Quasimodo, *Oboe sommerso*	
1933	Ignazio Silone, *Fontamara* Ungaretti, *Sentimento del tempo*	
1935		War in Abyssinia (1935-6)
1936		Spanish Civil War (1936-9) Rome-Berlin Axis
1937	Silone, *Pane e vino*	Death of Gramsci
1938	Emilio Lussu, *Un anno sull'altipiano*	Anti-semitic Racial Laws
1939	Montale, *Le occasioni*	Italian-German Pact of Steel Second World War
1940	Dino Buzzati, *Il deserto dei Tartari* Riccardo Bacchelli, *Il mulino del Po*	Italy enters war Campaigns in Greece, Africa, Russia (1940-43)
1941	Elio Vittorini, *Conversazione in Sicilia*	
1942	Quasimodo, *Ed è subito sera*	
1943		Mussolini ousted. Armistice with Allies Germany occupies Northern/Central Italy and sets up 'Salò' Republic. Resistance/Civil War (1943-5)
1944	Giacomo Debenedetti, *16 ottobre 1943*	
1945	Edoardo de Filippo, *Napoli milioniaria!* Carlo Levi, *Cristo si è fermato a Eboli* Curzio Malaparte, *Kaputt* Umberto Saba, *Il canzoniere* Vittorini, *Uomini e no*	Liberation Capture and execution of Mussolini Women given vote
1946		Referendum: Italy becomes a republic
1947	Anna Banti, *Artemisia* Italo Calvino, *Il sentiero dei nidi di ragno* Antonio Gramsci, *Lettere dal carcere* Primo Levi, *Se questo è un uomo* Vasco Pratolini, *Cronache di poveri amanti*	

Year	Italian literature	Italian history
1948	Elsa Morante, *Menzogna e sortilegio* Cesare Pavese, *La casa in collina*	Christian Democrats (DC) win first postwar elections
1950	Pavese, *La luna e i falò*	
1951	Moravia, *Il conformista*	
1952	Calvino, *Il visconte dimezzato*	
1953	Anna Maria Ortese, *Il mare non bagna Napoli* Mario Rigoni Stern, *Il sergente della neve*	
1954		Trieste returned to Italy
1955	Pier Paolo Pasolini, *Ragazzi di vita* Pratolini, *Metello*	Italy admitted to UN
1956		Crisis in PCI after revelations about Stalin and Soviet invasion of Hungary
1957	Calvino, *Il barone rampante* Carlo Emilio Gadda, *Quer pasticciaccio brutto de via Merulana* Morante, *L'isola di Arturo* Pasolini, *Le ceneri di Gramsci*	Treaty of Rome establishes EEC
1958	Giuseppe Tomasi di Lampedusa, *Il gattopardo*	'Economic miracle' (1958-63) Election of Pope John XXIII
1960		Protests and violence as neo-fascist MSI close to governing coalition
1961	Leonardo Sciascia, *Il giorno della civetta*	
1962	Giorgio Bassani, *Il giardino dei Finzi-Contini* Paolo Volponi, *Memoriale*	
1963	Alberto Arbasino, *Fratelli d'Italia* Gadda, *La cognizione del dolore* Natalia Ginzburg, *Lessico famigliare* Primo Levi, *La tregua*	Socialist Party (PSI) joins government in first centre-left coalition
1964	Luigi Meneghello, *I piccoli maestri*	Death of Togliatti
1965	Calvino, *Cosmicomiche*	
1966	Sciascia, *A ciascuno il suo*	
1968	Beppe Fenoglio, *Il partigiano Johnny* Pasolini, *Teorema*	Student protests
1969		'Autunno caldo' of industrial unrest Terrorism ('anni di piombo', 1969-80) Divorce law

Year	Italian literature	Italian history
1972	Calvino, *Le città invisibili* Dario Fo, *Morte accidentale di un anarchico*	
1973		Proposal of 'historic compromise' between PCI and DC
1974	Morante, *La storia* Sciascia, *Todo modo*	Divorce referendum
1975	Stefano D'Arrigo, *Horcynus Orca* Oriana Fallaci, *Lettera a un bambino mai nato* Primo Levi, *Il sistema periodico* Pasolini, *Lettere luterane* Saba, *Ernesto*	Abortion referendum Murder of Pasolini
1976	Vincenzo Consolo, *Il sorriso dell'ignoto marinaio*	
1978	Sciascia, *L'affaire Moro* Andrea Zanzotto, *Il Galateo in bosco*	Abduction and murder of Aldo Moro
1979	Calvino, *Se una notte d'inverno un viaggiatore* Manganelli, *Centuria*	
1980	Umberto Eco, *Il nome della rosa* Franscesca Sanvitale, *Madre e figlia* Pier Vittorio Tondelli, *Altri libertini*	Bologna train bomb kills 85
1981	Gesualdo Bufalino, *Diceria dell'untore* Andrea de Carlo, *Treno di panna*	P2 Masonic lodge scandal
1983	Daniele Del Giudice, *Lo stadio di Wimbledon*	Socialist Bettino Craxi head of government (until 1987)
1984	Attilio Bertolucci, *Camera da letto* Gianni Celati, *Narratori delle pianure*	PCI largest party in European elections
1985	Antonio Tabucchi, *Piccoli equivoci senza importanza* Tondelli, *Rimini*	
1986	Claudio Magris, *Danubio* Primo Levi, *I sommersi e i salvati*	Mafia 'maxi-trial'
1988	Umberto Eco, *Il pendolo di Foucault* Roberto Calasso, *Le nozze di Cadmo e di Armonia*	
1989	Tondelli, *Camere separate*	
1990	Dacia Maraini, *La lunga vita di Marianna Ucrìa* Salah Methnani, *Immigrato*	Foundation of 'Lega nord'
1991		PCI becomes PDS ('Partito democratico di sinistra')

Year	Italian literature	Italian history
1992	Elena Ferrante, *L'amore molesto* Pasolini, *Petrolio* Sebastiano Vassalli, *La chimera*	Tangentopoli: huge bribing scandal destroys DC Murder of anti-mafia magistrates Falcone and Borsellino
1993	Ortese, *Il cardillo addolorato*	
1994		Silvio Berlusconi founds 'Forza Italia', wins election and forms government for 8 months
1996	*Gioventù cannibale* (anthology) Alessandro Baricco, *Seta*	PDS and coalition win elections
1997	Carlo Lucarelli, *Almost Blue*	
1999	Andrea Camilleri, *La mossa del cavallo*	
2001	Niccolò Ammaniti, *Io non ho paura*	Second Berlusconi government

1

Foundations

This first chapter looks at three of the fundamental, underlying factors which have determined the shape of Italian literature in the twentieth century: geography, language, and the spaces of literary production.

1.1. Geography

1.1.1. Italy: national and local identities

Unlike France or Britain, with their centralised nation-states and grand, cosmopolitan capitals, Italy has had a deeply decentralised and fractured history and culture, divided as it was for nearly 1500 years from the fall of the Roman Empire until its unification in the nineteenth century (the 'Risorgimento'). To this day, dozens of cities and regions maintain the traditions, the architecture, the institutions and the civic pride (and the tourist trade) derived from more or less extended periods as separate fiefdoms or statelets in the past. Local government and business vigorously promote and subsidise local sites of tradition and heritage (museums, theatres and opera houses, libraries and universities, archives of local history and local writers, prestige exhibitions and publications), and broader cultural activity within each region. Such a patchwork of local identities, 'from below' as it were, has run alongside and complicated attempts since the Risorgimento to create and impose ('from above') a unified Italian national identity and culture. One consequence of this has been conflict and tension, most notably in the so-called 'Southern Question', the abyss of inequality and prejudice between North and South that has dogged Italy ever since unification; but regional diversity has also been a source of immense cultural vitality.

Literature has frequently been a privileged arena in which the negotiation between the local and the national has taken place. This is in part because culture invariably plays a crucial role in building the imaginary foundations (the myths, the visions of history and landscape, and so on) on which national identities are constructed. In Italy, this role for literature was paradoxically strengthened by the lack of national political unity: before unification, 'Italy' almost seemed to exist only in the patriotic laments of the great Italian writers from Dante, Petrarch and Machiavelli to Leopardi and Manzoni, and in the glories of the Roman Empire and Renaissance art. In the nineteenth century, high culture thus became one of the strongest vessels of the nation-in-the-making, in a heroic, Romantic sense. And after unification, literature continued to be used in patriotic and pedagogical ways – in street plaques and schools, for example – to maintain its official position within the national culture. Indeed, this is one reason at least why literature itself, and a rather traditional conception of its role and value, resisted the pressures of mass culture for longer in Italy than in some other European countries in the twentieth century (see Chapter 2).

Italian literature has, however, also always carried with it powerful resonances of the local. Questions of birthplace and origin continue to be fundamental in establishing style and literary identity. Thus, it would make little sense to read any of the following major writers of the century (and many others besides) without making substantial reference to the cities, regions or particular landscapes that permeate their work in different ways: Edoardo de Filippo (Naples), Grazia Deledda (Sardinia), Carlo Emilio Gadda (Milan, Rome), Carlo Levi (Basilicata and the South), Eugenio Montale (Liguria), Pier Paolo Pasolini (Friuli, Rome), Cesare Pavese (Turin and Piedmont), Vasco Pratolini (Florence), Ignazio Silone (the Abruzzi), Italo Svevo (Trieste), Andrea Zanzotto (the

Veneto). At times, this attachment of writers to place has led to their folklorisation, as each becomes a sort of local hero. But this is to limit the significance of their rootedness, to miss the point of the complicated balance between local identity and literary complexity. Thus Pavese's Piedmont was as much an adapted version of Hemingway's or Faulkner's America as an evocation of his real home; Gadda's Rome or Milan as much modernist webs of languages, idioms and mediations as representations of real cities; Pasolini's Friuli and Rome evolved over the course of his career into imaginary sites of authenticity and raw sexuality also charted in Morocco, Yemen and India. And, conversely, Italo Calvino's extraordinary, magical visions of cities in *Le città invisibili* ('Invisible Cities', 1972) turn out to have been dreamlike prisms of memories of the protagonist Marco Polo's hometown, Venice. As these examples suggest, place, as well as at times dragging literature back to folklore, also makes possible a rich fluidity and multiplicity of identities (local, national, universal, transversal).

1.1.2. Country, city, centres, margins, borders

Literary maps, then, are fundamental to our understanding of modern Italian literature; but we can draw our maps in different ways. Beyond linking writers to named places from their biography, we can mark out other, looser geographical categories or archetypes which help make some general (historical and cultural) sense of local specifics. A simple, but hugely important example for our purposes would be the pairing 'country' and 'city'. Simplifying greatly the complex tensions between the two, we can say that country and landscape often equate with tradition (and childhood) and city points to modernity (and adulthood). Thus, the persistent attachment of modern Italian literature to the former is one of the prime markers of its resistance to modernity (see Chapter 2.2.1).

Another important set of cultural-geographical archetypes underlying literary identity is found in the layered relations between centres, margins and borders. A good illustration is the contrasting fortunes of Florence and Trieste as cultural centres in the twentieth century.

Florence, of course, had been *the* centre of the Italian literary tradition (Dante, Petrarch, Boccaccio) and indeed of the Italian language (which was derived from Tuscan). In the early period of the twentieth century, this centrality looked set fair: a group of bold young writers (Giovanni Papini, Giuseppe Prezzolini, Ardengo Soffici, among others) created a vital project for cultural renewal in Florence, tapping into the latest philosophies and social realities. They produced brilliant journals, such as *Leonardo* (1903-7) and *La Voce* (1908-16), published journalism, essays and books, were in dialogue with the greatest philosopher of the day, Benedetto Croce. They met in bars such as the famous 'Giubbe rosse' and flirted with avant-garde trends, such as Futurism (Papini and Soffici ran a Futurist journal, *Lacerba*, in 1913-14). The energy emanating from Florence acted like a magnet, and a number of aspiring young Triestine writers (Umberto Saba, Scipio Slataper, Gianni Stuparich) looked to Florence as a path to Italianisation (Trieste was not yet part of Italy) and to modern ideas, from their marginal outpost. At the same time, Italo Svevo, who was to emerge as by far the most important Triestine writer of the century, struggled to be recognised in Italy, snubbed because his Italian was more than a little tinged with local usage and thus not quite standard literary Florentine.

Florence's status as a centre of cultural vitality was not to last, however. Although the legacy of the *Voce* generation continued to draw writers to the city (Montale lived there between 1927 and 1948; Gadda between 1940 and 1950), to produce interesting journals during the Fascist era (e.g. *Solaria*) and to give a Tuscan tinge to Fascist cultural debates (e.g. in the ruralist so-called 'Strapaese' group of the 1920s), over the course of the postwar period its importance faded. Relatively speaking, Trieste fared better, coming to seem ever closer to the centre of what modern or postmodern culture represents, with its hybridity, marginality, its status as a crossing-point of Italian and Central European cultures.

In comparison, the canonical and established traditions of Florence seem staid and provincial. The complete transformation of Svevo's reputation is one strong indicator of this reversal, but perhaps the epitome of the Triestine trend is the contemporary academic and intellectual Claudio Magris, who achieved international success with his beguiling meditation-cum-travelogue on the geographical lifeblood of *Mitteleuropa*, the river Danube (*Danubio*, 'Danube', 1986).

Florence and Trieste neatly illustrate the importance of the network of centres, margins and borders that characterise the cultural geography of Italy, and the ways in which that geography can shift over time. It can also be seen at work 'vertically', within single geographical and social spaces, as seen for example in the Roman novels and poems of Pier Paolo Pasolini. In a 1950s poem called 'L'Appennino' ('The Appennine'), Pasolini moves in a grand sweep on Rome, the seat of the Catholic Church (and so of both spiritual and political power), while eyeing the poor underclasses in the slums at the city's edge, described as an army of the marginalised, '[...] nell'attesa/ di farsi cristiano nella cristiana/ città' (waiting/ to become Christian in the Christian/ city). The same geographical-cum-theological metaphor appeared in the title of Carlo Levi's famous memoir of his 1930s exile in the South, *Cristo si è fermato a Eboli* ('Christ Stopped at Eboli', 1945).

1.1.3. Place and cultural production

A further sense in which geography can be factored into literature is through the geographical sociology of literary production and literary history. Here our two examples will be Turin and Sicily.

Turin, like all Italian cities, has its own very particular identity and history. Historically, it was the first capital of Italy and seat of the royal family. In the twentieth century, it evokes images of Fiat car factories, the newspaper *La stampa* and the football team *Juventus*, all owned by the hugely powerful, patrician family, the Agnellis; and it also evokes the strikes and mass politicisation of the workers who manned Fiat's factories. But Turin also made striking contributions to the cultural life of the century, in two directions in particular. First, there was an extraordinary flourishing in the early decades of the century of a local intelligentsia, ranging from the Communist left to liberal-left anti-Fascists. Out of these circles in the fervid politics of the early part of the century emerged figures such as the Communist leader and later influential Marxist theorist Antonio Gramsci, the liberal Piero Gobetti (who died young, the victim of a beating), Luigi Einaudi (economist and postwar President of Italy), and many others. The liberal anti-Fascist movement 'Giustizia e libertà' ('Justice and Freedom') was founded here and drew in a series of future writers who would do much to shape Italian literature of the middle decades of the century (among them Cesare Pavese, Natalia Ginzburg, Carlo Levi and Primo Levi). Beyond literature, these groupings included figures such as the political philosopher Norberto Bobbio or the unionist and writer Vittorio Foa, who survived to the end of the century and took on roles akin to the moral conscience of the nation.

There was, however, a further, narrower factor propelling Turin's intelligentsia into a powerfully influential position in the literary-intellectual life of Italy in the mid-twentieth century. This was the Einaudi publishing house, founded in 1933 by the son of Luigi, Giulio. Begun on a small scale, Einaudi gradually drew many of the leading lights of Turin's anti-Fascist intellectuals. Pavese and Natalia Ginzburg's husband Leone (tortured to death by the Nazis in a Rome prison in 1944) were determining influences on its original lists in literature, especially translated literature, history and philosophy. The group expanded to Rome and, after the war, to Milan also, becoming close to the Communist Party (PCI). As part of this expansion, it published Elio Vittorini's extraordinarily vital journal of new ideas *Politecnico* (1945-47). The close collaboration, as editors and advisers, of several important writers set its mark on Einaudi and in turn on postwar Italian literature. Pavese was perhaps the crucial figure until his suicide in 1950; in the 1950s, Vittorini oversaw an imprint called 'I gettoni' which published many important young writers for the first time; and Italo Calvino also became a crucial figure at Einaudi, guiding, advising and overseeing many writers, a role as important in shaping the directions of postwar Italian narrative as his own highly influential *oeuvre*. Indeed, Einaudi's list now reads like an élite rollcall of postwar Italian literature (Pavese, Vittorini, Ginzburg, Calvino, Fenoglio, Cassola, Sciascia, Fortini, Morante, Primo Levi; and in theatre both Edoardo de Filippo and Dario Fo). At least as important as these literary figures, however, were the collaborative culture of the editorial business, with its group meetings and consultations over publishing decisions, and also Einaudi's grand 'encyclopaedic' projects from the 1970s onwards, such as the multi-volume reference works *Letteratura italiana* ('Italian Literature') and *Storia d'Italia* ('History of Italy'). Einaudi was for a time an intellectually coherent and powerful source of ideas from the left in the postwar period and, before a sharp decline in the 1980s leading to a near-terminal crisis, its authority sustained Turin as a key cultural centre, even as Rome and Milan otherwise overshadowed it. It gave the city a sort of 'virtual' cultural space and identity.

Einaudi was far from alone as a publisher creating a cultural project rooted in a certain place: Benedetto Croce stamped his authoritative identity on the Laterza publisher in Bari; Giangiacomo Feltrinelli launched the creatively left-wing publisher of that name in Milan in the 1950s, mixing glamour and radicalism; Adelphi, founded in Milan in 1962, gathered around it an aura of central European sophistication and myth, not least through its flagship project of publishing in Italian translation the work of the nineteenth-century German philosopher, Nietzsche. All these houses exist at an interface between their commercial operation and their cultural capital, standing for a particular kind of writing and originating in a particular place, both real and symbolic.

Our second example shows real and symbolic geography at work in a slightly different sense, creating a thread of literary history. As we saw earlier, 'Triestinità' became in retrospect a strongly identifiable regional identity in modern Italian literature, in a line drawn from Claudio Magris back towards the work of Svevo, Saba and others and set in relation to the national tradition. Here place lies at the origin of a set of literary issues shared by an extended body of literary work, so that a sort of semi-autonomous micro-tradition emerges from within the larger national literature. Certainly, the richest example of such a micro-tradition in modern Italian literature – akin in force and vitality to the case of Irish writing (Shaw, Yeats, Joyce, Beckett) within the modern English tradition – is Sicilian literature.

The strength and depth of modern Sicilian literature is remarkable: rooted in the generation of Giovanni Verga and the Sicilian realist writers (or 'veristi') of the late nineteenth century, the modern Sicilian canon would include Luigi Pirandello, Salvatore Quasimodo, Vitaliano Brancati, Elio Vittorini, Giuseppe Tomasi di Lampedusa, Leonardo Sciascia, Vincenzo Consolo and Gesualdo Bufalino, down to the contemporary bestselling writer of Sicilian detective stories, Andrea Camilleri. With each of these, a sense of place, language and landscape, and often the memory of it (as with the Irish writers, many left Sicily behind) is crucial to an understanding of their work.

The factor of literary production is also pertinent here: local publishers such as Sellerio in Palermo (founded in 1969) forged a strong local image and identity, publishing works by many of the writers listed above. The power and substance of modern Sicilian literature within the history of Italian literature is of another order, however. It derives from a cluster of problems, images and motifs which address Sicily, its history and its specificity, and which recur within and between the works of these different writers. And questions of 'Sicilianness' also pose questions about the Italian national identity against which Sicilianness inevitably defines itself: Italy categorises Sicily and Sicilian culture as marginal, subaltern and, on occasion, simply inferior, defining its culture and identity through this process of marginalisation and exclusion. But if Sicilianness and Italianness often stand apparently in antithesis, they can also turn out to be veiled images each of the other. Thus, the famous description in Tomasi di Lampedusa's masterly novel, *Il gattopardo* ('The Leopard', 1958), of a Sicily in a permanent state of sleep born of millennia of invasion and occupation ostensibly works as an explanation of Sicily's inability to respond to the new unified Italy; but in a veiled sense, it also speaks of the larger history of the Italian peninsula, also unable to awaken from so many centuries of foreign rule and self-forgetting: ' "Il sonno, caro Chevalley, il sonno è ciò che i Siciliani vogliono, ed essi odieranno sempre chi li vorrà svegliare [...] la nostra sensualità è desiderio di oblio, le schioppet-tate e le coltellate nostre, desiderio di morte; desiderio di immobilità voluttuosa, cioè ancora di morte, la nostra pigrizia [...]" ' ('Sleep, my dear Chevalley, sleep is what Sicilians want, and they will hate for ever anyone who tries to wake them [...] our sensuality is a desire for oblivion, our stabbings and shooting a desire for death; and our laziness no more than a desire for a voluptuous immobility, in other words again, for death [...]').

This is one of the senses in which Sciascia famously spoke of Sicily as a metaphor as much as a geographical location (*La Sicilia come metafora*, 'Sicily as Metaphor', 1979), as a blend of the real and the mythical. Recurrent moments, anxieties, images and motifs act as the glue to bind together Sicilian literature, constantly in dia-logue with itself. These include the myth (and stereotype) of Sicily as mysterious, dark, inscrutable and immoveable; and the image of Sicily as sensual, sexual, primitive and dangerous. Both Pirandello and Brancati dedicated several novels and plays to the contrasting power in Sicily between the impulses of desire and the body, the codified actions or duties associated with masculinity and feminin-ity, and the social constraints and strictures on both provided by the local honour code. The contradictions that ensue often lead to violent conflict, whether represented in comic or (melo)dramatic tone. And in turn, honour, violence and danger point to a final theme of Sicilian literature, emerging only in the second half of the century (even if the phenomenon was born in the later nineteenth century): that of the 'mafia', and the code of silence (or 'omertà') that protects it.

1.2. Language

Links between language and literature, and from these to the culture history and politics of the nation as a whole, are pivotal features of any national literature; in the case of Italy, they form a particularly complex web of relations.

As with the geography of Italy, the key characteristic of the Italian language (or rather languages) is its diversity. Alongside standard Italian (derived from Tuscan), there are distinct regional varieties of standard Italian, and innumerable discrete localised languages known as dialects. Each of these forms is permeable, influencing and inflecting the others. Each finds expression in modern literature, in a wide variety of linguistic hybrids and mixes, even as standard Italian dominates (not surprisingly, since the standard was in large part shaped by the language of the literary canon).

Dialects have conventionally been treated as 'minor' or 'lower' forms of Italian, less stable and more oral than written in usage. Nevertheless, there is an extraordinarily rich and complex field of dialect literature (especially in poetry and theatre) that runs alongside, intersects and illuminates the history of literature in standard Italian, especially in the second half of the twentieth century. Dialect literature early in the century tended towards a folkloric, impressionistic poetry of landscape and local colour, or an expression of local 'low' traditions, most famously illustrated by the Neapolitan comic theatre. The Fascist regime, officially at least, clamped down on dialect usage in general. In postwar generations, however, there was a return to dialect as a vital resource for linguistic renewal, as an expression of private and communal identity and as a means for subversion of literary conventions, whether for ideological reasons or avant-garde aesthetic reasons, or both (Pasolini was a key figure here, influenced by earlier poets such as Biagio Marin and Delio Tessa). Later in the century, in the work of poets such as Zanzotto or Franco Loi, or the trend known as 'poesia neo-dialettale', dialects paradoxically found themselves deployed as exclusive, isolated and highly literary languages, as they faded as real, spoken languages on the ground.

Perhaps even more important than dialect literature as such were the ways in which dialectal elements, Italianised versions of dialect and regional varieties of Italian fed their way into otherwise standard literary Italian, in phonology, lexicon and syntax, as markers of place, immediacy, or aesthetic hybridity. Verga inserted some dialect or regional words and local proverbs (in Italianised forms) into his Sicilian narratives and this realist trend recurred in certain 'Neo-Realist' writers of the 1940s and 1950s, as they tried to capture the oral patterns of speech of their narrative milieux. Pasolini's Roman novels of the 1950s (*Ragazzi di vita*, 'Boys on the Make',1955; *Una vita violenta*, 'A Violent Life', 1958) took this slang- and dialect-driven realism to a new extreme. But the stronger legacy of this tradition was perhaps to be found in a broader shift towards orality, rather than towards dialect narrowly speaking, as is well illustrated in the work of Gianni Celati (e.g. *Narratori delle pianure*, 'Storytellers of the Plains', 1984) and also in the youth-driven narratives of 1990s writers such as Enrico Brizzi. A certain line of Italian lyric poetry, also, following in the footsteps of d'Annunzio and Pascoli, has made rich use of localised, regionally-specific vocabulary, especially that of landscape and nature.

Standard Italian, then, in its literary expression, has constantly been open to variation and renewal through contact with dialects and regional varieties. Running in tension with this openness, however, has been its historical conservatism and elitism. As noted, Tuscan was chosen as the national language after unification, largely thanks to its rich literary history and prestige. It struggled for a century to establish itself as a genuinely national language and, for a long period, only a minority of the population knew, let alone spoke or wrote regularly in Italian. Literary Italian, therefore, brought with it an aura of authority, beauty and pedagogical worth, but was to a significant degree cut off from the language of the world around it. Where it did have contact with the non-literary language, it was from a sort of 'top-down' position, engaged in shaping an ideal, beautiful language or teaching how to write 'properly', rather than reflecting 'bottom-up', real and changing language use. And indeed, an influential core of twentieth-century Italian literature was founded in a literary language that was elevated, rich, formal, lyrical, above and beyond the common-place: for example, the neo-classical, syntactically complex and highly imaged prose of the 1920s known as 'prosa d'arte' (practised by figures such as Vincenzo Cardarelli and Emilio Cecchi); and the poetry of Montale, Giuseppe Ungaretti, Mario Luzi and others, which was labelled 'hermetic' for being obscure and indecipher-able. Even in the late twentieth century, many novels strove to create an exclusive aura for literature through a language rich in subjective, evocative lyricism and abstraction (e.g. in the work of Alessandro Baricco).

Many literary innovations of the twentieth century were, how-ever, devoted to reversing this 'hermetic' trend, shifting literary language towards the languages and idioms of real voices, or at least away from the enclosed formalities assumed to be proper to literature. This meant either capturing the rhythms and cadences of spoken language in writing as noted above, or forging a written language of lucid, concise directness, stripped of the acrobatics of traditional rhetoric or lyricism (in writers such as Primo Levi, Italo Calvino and Umberto Eco).

By the later decades of the century, these efforts at inclusive innovation in the literary language seemed to be succeeding, but only in time to be overtaken by other, deeper changes. By the time standard Italian was established as overwhelmingly the first lan-guage of the Italians, roughly a century after unification (although even in 1996, only a third of Italians spoke *only* standard Italian), the voices of literature had become marginal. A genuinely national language was the product of mass education and mass literacy, migration and the new media of the post-Second-World-War era, not of patrician pedagogy. In 1964, in an essay entitled 'Nuove questioni linguistiche' ('New Linguistic Questions'), Pasolini famously lamented the new Italian born of a deadly combination of commercial-industrial jargon, homogenising consumerism and TV chatter. Thirty-five years on, in 1996, the publishing phenomenon of the year was an anthology of so-called 'cannibal' writers (e.g. Niccolò Ammaniti, Aldo Nove), whose violent, hyperactive idiom was born of the new media, from MTV to Stephen King and contemporary Hollywood films. As the 'cannibali' suggest, perhaps at least as important as the balance between Italian, regional variety and dialect in twentieth-century literary Italian, are, on the one hand, the balance between formal written language and oral, colloquial language, and, on the other hand, the balance between language itself and the noise of audio-visual, mass-media modernity.

1.3. Spaces

1.3.1. Cultural operators

As well as in relation to place and to language, literature is also to be located in particular spaces within a given society, that is, the sites, networks and institutions from where writers typically operate. Charting the different spaces of literature, each with their own rules and conditions, amounts to an alternative vision of the history of literature itself. So, for example, it might be said that the 'court' was the space that defined and produced the characteristic literature of the Renaissance; or that the 'coffee-house' defined and produced some of the key works of the Enlightenment, from London to Venice to Milan; and similarly for the medieval 'piazza' or the nineteenth-century literary 'salon'. The court, the coffee-house, the piazza and the salon were all to differing degrees regulated spaces where literary and intellectual dialogue occurred, leading more or less directly to the production of literary works, and also to the dissemination of a representative type or cultural figure (respectively, the courtier, the *philosophe* or scribbler, the jester or preacher, the *littérateur*). In these spaces, these figures meet each other, their patrons and their audience. In the twentieth century, three such spaces suggest themselves: the school or university, the publishing house and the newspaper or media generally. And if we were to choose a label for the type or figure of the modern writer found at work in these spaces, it would be something like the 'the intellectual' or what Italians call the 'cultural operator'.

Each of the three spaces (in education, publishing and the media) had its own history and evolution over the course of the century, as institutions, businesses and cultural industries. Writers adopted different positions within them, whose nuances would be too many to identify simply, although we could, for example, note the strong bias towards a humanities-based as opposed to a scientific culture in all of them. Many writers had little or nothing to do with them; but even the apparent exceptions tended to prove the rule. Take Primo Levi, who worked in an industrial paint company and was an outsider to the literary establishment, but who nevertheless did write for *La stampa* regularly, frequently gave talks at schools, and had a fair amount of professional contact with his publishing house, Einaudi.

Perhaps the overriding characteristic of the cultural operator is to move eclectically between various spaces, cobbling together an income and prestige through, say, occasional seminars at a university, commissioned journalism and book reviewing or opinion pieces for the cultural pages of a newspaper, perhaps writing a screenplay, as well as acting as a consultant to a publisher on a list of modern poetry, translating some of the poets herself, or editing an anthology of travel writing, and sitting on the jury of a prestigious literary prize. In between all of these, our imaginary writer might be finishing her latest novel and corresponding with a close-knit circle of fellow writers about the future of literature.

If this made-up example seems too eclectic, take the real example of the Nobel prize-winning poet Eugenio Montale: as well as writing his relatively slim output of poetry between 1925 (*Ossi di seppia*, 'Cuttlefish Bones') and 1977 (*Quaderno di quattro anni*, 'Notebook of Four Years', the last collection published during his lifetime), Montale also wrote literary criticism extensively beginning in the 1920s; worked for the Florentine publisher Bemporad after 1927; was director of the prestigious Florentine cultural institute the 'Gabinetto Vieusseux' between 1929 and 1938 (he was sacked for political reasons); was an active contributor to and sometime editor of literary-cultural journals both before and after the war (e.g. *Solaria*, 1926-34; *Il mondo*, 1945-7); translated literature from English, French and Spanish (at times relying on the anonymous work of others); and after 1948 became a long-term regular contributor to the Milan newspaper *Il corriere della sera*, writing essays, book reviews, travel reportage and, especially, music and opera reviews.

In all this activity, a distinction often needs to be made between paid work and work which shapes and conditions a writer's literary output; but the distinction and the hierarchy is inevitably blurred. Take the example of journalism: Anna Maria Ortese worked in journalism as a way of earning a basic wage, combining reportage with powerful expressionistic intensity in her 1953 book *Il mare non bagna Napoli* ('The Sea Does Not Bathe Naples'), and fed this into the extraordinary visionary-fantastic style of her later fiction; and Italo Calvino built up his quizzical, philosophical last book *Palomar* ('Palomar', 1983) out of a series of topical newspaper pieces for *Il corriere della sera* and *La repubblica*.

The example of cinema is even more striking: a very large number of writers over the century worked for the cinema (Verga, d'Annunzio, Pirandello, Moravia, Brancati, Soldati, Flaiano, Bassani, Pasolini, Pratolini; and more), mostly on screenplays and mostly for money, but there was an inevitable impact on their work as writers, in the way they told stories and constructed fictional worlds, in their ways of perceiving and seeing, and in their rhythms of production. The same could be said in certain periods for both radio and television.

Certain of the spaces of modern literature have also, inevitably, become material for fiction itself, as writers spent more and more time within them; just as, say, Castiglione made the court and its courtier the topic of his *Cortegiano* ('Courtier') in sixteenth-century

Urbino. Sibilla Aleramo's important autobiographical novel *Una donna* ('A Woman', 1906), for example, ends with a description of the economic and psychological emancipation of the protagonist who leaves her family to move to Rome and to work in journals, newspapers and feminist activism (on women's writing, see Chapter 6.2 below). And two of the most successful novels of recent decades – Italo Calvino's *Se una notte d'inverno un viaggiatore* ('If on a Winter's Night a Traveller', 1979) and Umberto Eco's *Il pendolo di Foucault* ('Foucault's Pendulum', 1988) – are both partly set within the world of publishing, and do much to satirise and play games with the work that goes on there.

1.3.2. Journals and other projects

As well as filtering through to writers' individual literary *oeuvres* in a number of different ways, the spaces of literature also facilitated particular kinds of groupings and networks between writers, in anything from concerted intellectual projects or movements (such as Futurism) to looser collaborations. The characteristic group literary project in twentieth-century Italy was the literary journal. I have already mentioned examples of how a moment in literary history is often best encapsulated in a usually short-lived, innovative, small-circulation journal: *La Voce* (and *Lacerba*) in early twentieth-century Florence, or Vittorini's *Politecnico* in postwar Milan; and there were any number of others, from the rich array of cultural journals of the Fascist period (e.g. *Solaria*, 1926-34; *900 (Novecento)*, 1926-29; *Primato*, 1940-43); to *Quindici* (1967-69), one of several journals crucial to the 1968 student movements; or the literary magazine *Panta*, launched by Pier Vittorio Tondelli and others in 1990 to promote new narrative by young writers (modelled in name and content on the English magazine *Granta*).

These last two examples both emerged out of one of our key spaces of literature, the university, but from the position of students rather than professor-intellectuals. They are indicative of another intensely important context for literature at various points during the century, the generational context which recast culture as youth culture, from *La Voce* through to the anti-globalisation movements of the very end of the century (see Chapter 6.3).

Literary journals were invariably set up and run autonomously by the writers themselves, perhaps with the commercial support of a publisher, for the express purpose of creating a space for a certain intellectual project. Other cultural institutions were set up and controlled from beyond the strictly literary sphere. A quite exceptional example in Italy was that of the Olivetti typewriter and later electronics business, based in Ivrea in Northern Italy, owned by the socialist entrepreneur Adriano Olivetti, which from the 1950s ran a research institute and journal called 'Comunità', promoting radical new work in sociology, urban planning, architecture, design; and employing important intellectuals and literary figures such as Franco Fortini and Paolo Volponi in the process. On another level, throughout the century, the Church played a fundamental role in acting as a capillary cultural organisation with its own local networks, magazines and parish cinemas (and its own system of censorship).

1.3.3. The state

Commonly, the public institutions of culture were state-run, or at least state-funded. This is a particularly fraught issue for twentieth-century Italy since for a 21-year period, between 1922 and 1943, the state was run by Mussolini's Fascist régime. As enthusiastic, if not always successful centralisers and institutionalisers, the Fascists set up a number of bodies to control and monitor the spaces of culture, while at the same time adopting a relatively flexible attitude to the different artistic projects competing for attention in the 1920s and 1930s, which meant that the space for non-Fascist culture was surprisingly large. What mattered to the régime was the control of the distribution of culture, its use for the indirect manufacture of consent, and the benefits of prestige and pomp gleaned from its grander manifestations. Examples of institutions or spaces for culture set up by the Fascists include the 'Reale Accademia d'Italia', 'The Royal Academy of Italy' (set up in 1925; Pirandello and Marinetti were among the members), the *Enciclopedia italiana* project (1929-39) (although this was markedly less 'Fascistic' than other projects), a Fascist institute of culture, a Fascist writers' union, and so on. But it also included the mass organisations of women, the young and workers, which became channels for controlling the distribution of cultural material.

It is striking to note that the régime intervened with particular force in each of our three characteristic spaces for literature: school and university (one of the first major Fascist reforms was of schools, under the aegis of the philosopher Giovanni Gentile; all but a handful of universities professors took an oath of loyalty in 1931; students were corralled into movements (GUF and GIL) which ran cultural events, magazines and prizes); newspapers and the media (Mussolini had been a journalist and a newspaper editor, and his régime increasingly controlled and occupied the press and other media); and publishing (the state financed publication of journals, magazines, textbooks and the like, and controlled all other publishing through the office of the censor).

Although the fall of the Fascist régime spelled the definitive end of the totalitarian project of containing and controlling all spheres of the state and nation in Italy, there were nevertheless lines of continuity in state-culture relations from Fascist to democratic Italy. The state continued to fund a large number of cultural products, institutions, prizes and the like, and to monitor and censor them (with decreasing vigour over time). And just as the Church worked as a network of cultural formation and dissemination, so, after the war, political parties began to fulfil the same role, with the Communist Party (PCI) in particular setting up an extensive cultural network. The PCI sponsored journals and magazines, ran its own daily newspaper (*L'Unità*), and its local and national cultural festivals (the 'feste dell'Unità'), had own publisher (Editori

Riuniti) as well as the support of others such as Feltrinelli, and generally drew many writers and intellectuals towards it as members or so-called 'fellow travellers'.

*

Looking at the spaces and institutions of literature means looking at the ways in which writers entered the public sphere in the twentieth century (see Chapter 5). To complement everything said so far, it is important to consider also how readers entered that same sphere, where and how they came into contact with literary culture. Many of the same areas would emerge again: changes in the media (newspapers, radio, cinema, TV) and the extraordinary advances in education over the century (first in basic literacy, then in full school and university education on a mass scale), created at least the potential for a mass readership with the tools to enjoy and critically engage with literature for the first time, and provided a context for the 'pedagogical' tendencies of the cultural operator. An extraordinary example of this potential confluence occurred in the very first years of the twenty-first century, when major national newspapers (*La repubblica, Il corriere della sera*) began selling cheap literary classics bundled in with the daily paper, with introductory essays by famous writers-cum-cultural operators. In a country with notoriously low rates of newspaper- and book-reading, this semi-commercial, semi-pedagogical initiative was a runaway success, selling over 25 million works of 'great literature' in one year alone.

Selected reading

To read further on the general factors influencing the production of twentieth-century Italian literature and on twentieth-century Italian history and culture in general, the following survey and reference works are good places to start:

In English

Zygmunt Baranski and Rebecca West (eds), *Modern Italian Culture* (Cambridge: Cambridge University Press, 2001).

Norberto Bobbio, *Ideological Profile of Twentieth-Century Italy* (Princeton: Princeton University Press, 1995). Modern Italian political thought, as seen by the authoritative liberal philosopher.

Peter Brand and Lino Pertile (eds), *The Cambridge History of Italian Literature* (Cambridge: Cambridge University Press, 1997). See especially chs 35-44.

Martin Clark, *Modern Italy 1871-1995* (London: Longman, 1996). Standard survey of Italian history since Unification.

Jonathan Davis (ed.), *Short Oxford History of Italy* (Oxford: Oxford University Press, 2000 onwards). See especially vols 6 and 7, *Liberal and Fascist Italy* and *Italy since 1945*.

John Foot, *Modern Italy* (London: Palgrave, 2002). Thematic history of the century, focusing on 'nation', 'state', 'economy and society' and 'politics'.

David Forgacs, *Italian Culture in the Industrial Era: 1910-1980* (Manchester: Manchester University Press, 1990). Focuses on mass culture (newspapers, radio, TV, publishing, cinema).

David Forgacs and Robert Lumley (eds), *Italian Cultural Studies* (Oxford: Oxford University Press, 1996).

Paul Ginsborg, *History of Contemporary Italy* (Harmondsworth: Penguin,1990). Authoritative history of postwar Italy with interest in sociology as well as politics.

Peter Hainsworth and David Robey (eds), *The Oxford Companion to Italian Literature* (Oxford: Oxford University Press, 2002). Useful dictionary format.

Anna Laura Lepschy and Giulio Lepschy, *The Italian Language Today* (London: Routledge, 1988).

Gino Moliterno (ed.), *Encyclopedia of Contemporary Italian Culture* (London: Routledge, 2000).

In Italian

Alberto Asor Rosa (ed.), *Letteratura italiana* (Turin: Einaudi, 1982-96). Influential encyclopedic work. Available on CD-ROM.

Giulio Ferroni, *Storia della letteratura italiana. Il novecento* (Turin: Einaudi, 1991). A very thorough survey written for Italian students.
Corrado Stajano (ed.), *La cultura italiana del Novecento* (Bari: Laterza, 1996).

2

Tradition

This book is primarily interested in Italian literature's encounter with modernity. But as we explore the different forms this encounter took, we need to bear in mind all the while the countervailing forces, pulling away from the modern, towards tradition and continuity with the past. The pull of tradition persisted with remarkable tenacity through the twentieth century, fed in part by the conservatism of the literary élite (and perhaps of literature *per se*) and by the weighty legacy of past glories (Ancient Rome, the Renaissance); and in part by an engaged, cultural and ideological resistance to what modernity represented. This chapter looks at some examples of the persistence of tradition in the century's literary culture.

2.1. Modernity, tradition, intervention

A good starting-point would be the terms modernity and tradition themselves. First of all, we should note their co-dependence: competing impulses towards modernity and tradition often co-existed with an almost schizophrenic simultaneity at the very heart of the culture and politics of modern Italy. Take the crucial example of the complex cultural politics of the Fascist régime. The cultural arbiters of Fascism (including Mussolini himself) somehow managed to embrace both high modernist and neo-classical art, investing in myths of progress and technology, on the one hand, and myths of Ancient Rome, on the other. Writers and artists competed to have their work, whether modernist or traditionalist, approved as the official expression of Fascist art. (In this Fascism was strikingly unlike Nazi Germany, where cultural politics were singleminded and dogmatic in the extreme.) And Fascism was not unique in this respect in modern Italy: parallel confusions and anxieties surrounding traditional culture and the modern existed within the Marxist cultural sphere of the postwar Communist Party (PCI).

As these examples suggest, we also need to be wary here of the fraught and often mismatched relationship between politics and culture in the twentieth century. In both spheres, terms such as modernity or progress, and their opposites tradition or reaction, were 'spun' to mean profoundly different things. Vittorini famously fell out publicly in 1947 with the leader of the PCI, Palmiro Togliatti, over the meaning of Communist, modern progress. Vittorini objected to attempts from the party to impose a line, Soviet-style, on his journal *Politecnico*, arguing instead for the autonomy of culture: 'the line that separates progress from reaction in the field of culture is not exactly the same line as separates them in politics'. Vittorini's struggle for independence from the PCI party line was also a struggle between his instinct for innovation and modernisation in the journal's make-up and Togliatti's instinctive cultural traditionalism.

A similar set of problems arises with the term 'modernism'. It might be tempting to assume that modernism – a label commonly used to denote a broad series of experimental changes in European art and literature of the late nineteenth and early twentieth centuries – was the aesthetic embodiment of the socio-economic and cultural modernisation going on around it. In reality, the relation was far from simple or untroubled: modernism was as much a reaction of the cultural élite *against* the modern world, with its threatening masses, as it was an open expression of it.

There are, then, several possible sources of confusion in trying to separate out modernisers from traditionalists in literature. They coexist within single movements and moments, indeed within single writers. They are ideologically inconsistent: both left and right are both modernising and conservative. And they have overlapping but confusingly different sets of meanings in the spheres of art, politics, or society at large. We can, however, suggest a useful rule-of-thumb distinction between a literature concerned with modernity and a literature drawn to tradition. Both Fascists and Marxists, their ideologues and their fellow-travellers in the cultural élite, perceived a need to *intervene* in the sphere of culture, to define and make anew Italian literature and art, as part of a redefinition of the Italian nation and society. Such interventionism, in all its different forms, is a plausible marker of literature's plunge into modernity.

Two contrasting literary movements illustrate the point about this cultural interventionism: first, Futurism, launched in 1909 in Paris and in Milan by Filippo Tommaso Marinetti, perhaps the first fully-fledged, totalising avant-garde artistic movement in Europe, dedicated to singing the praises of all things modern; and secondly, Neo-Realism, a loose grouping of committed writers, intellectuals, artists and filmmakers who tapped into the raw, popular euphoria of the anti-Fascist Resistance (1943-45) to help forge a new democratic Italy after 1945. It was the Neo-Realists (following the French philosopher Jean-Paul Sartre) who made common currency of the term 'impegno' (commitment) to describe the ethical and political interventionism of the contemporary writer.

As a result of their politics and their aesthetics, Futurism and Neo-Realism contained profoundly different visions of modernity – the former's violently nationalistic, proto-Fascist, and technology-driven; the latter's popular, progressive, mostly leftist and equality-driven – but both attempted actively to reshape their worlds. Both combined a critique of the present and the past – the Futurists simply dustbinning anything associated with the past; the Neo-Realists attempting a more articulated critique of contemporary poverty, inequality and injustice – with a more or less loosely utopian vision of the future – the Futurists envisioned a wholesale 'ricostruzione futurista dell'universo' (Futurist reconstruction of the universe), as a 1915 manifesto had it; the Neo-Realists occasionally envisioned a future without injustice, as in a famous scene in Rossellini's 1945 film *Roma città aperta* ('Rome Open City') in which two protagonists dream of the harmonious future they are risking their lives for in fighting the Nazis. Both also set great store by refashioning the forms and means of communication of art and literature, seeing this formal renewal as a principal means to the larger social renewal they sought.

If the interventionism in both Futurism and Neo-Realism had utopian dimensions, interventionism elsewhere took on darker, anti-modern forms. Certain figures, labelled by Umberto Eco in a famous 1964 essay 'apocalyptics', intervened only to mount loud assaults on all that modernity represented. By far the most famous and influential 'apocalyptic' voice in modern Italian culture was that of Pier Paolo Pasolini, in the years leading up to his murder in 1975, when he railed with extraordinary force and resonance against the homogenising, corrupting, fascistic power of the consumer society, symbolised in one famous article by the disappearance of fireflies from the Italian countryside (*Lettere luterane*, 'Lutheran Letters', 1975; *Scritti corsari*, 'Pirate Writings', 1976). But he was by no means the first: early in the century, a Triestine writer called Carlo Michelstaedter, shortly before committing suicide at the age of 23, wrote a dense but powerful treatise, *La persuasione e la rettorica* ('Persuasion and Rhetoric', 1913), which, through a strange web of quotations from ancient philosophy and meditations on being, denounced the fake, artificial and illusory 'rhetoric' that degraded the world around him, obfuscating authenticity and self-awareness. Even the lightly ironic Italo Svevo ended his great novel *La coscienza di Zeno* ('Zeno's Consciousness' or 'Zeno's Conscience', 1923) with an apocalyptic vision of the technological destruction of the world:

> Forse traverso una catastrofe inaudita prodotta dagli ordigni ritorneremo alla salute. Quando i gas velenosi non basteranno piú, un uomo fatto come tutti gli altri, nel segreto di una stanza di questo mondo, inventerà un esplosivo incomparabile […] Ed un altro

uomo fatto anche lui come tutti gli altri, ma degli altri un po' piú ammalato, ruberà tale esplosivo e s'arrampicherà al centro della terra per porlo nel punto ove il suo effetto può essere il massimo. Ci sarà un'esplosione enorme che nessuno udrà e la terra ritornata alla forma di nebulosa errerà nel cielo priva di parassiti e di malattie.

(Perhaps we will return to good health by way of an unprecedented catastrophe brought about by such devices. When poison gases will no longer be enough, a man like any other, hidden away in a room somewhere in the world, will invent an incomparable explosive [...] And another man also like any other, but a little sicker than the others, will steal this explosive and scramble to the centre of the earth to place it where its effect will be greatest. There will be an immense explosion that no one will hear and the earth, restored to its nebulous form, will wander the heavens shorn of all parasites and illnesses.)

Interestingly, both Svevo's (or Zeno's) catastrophic return to nature and Pasolini's fireflies prefigure first anti-nuclear and then ecological visions of the second half of the century.

Apocalyptics intervene to attack the modern in 'dystopian' rather than utopian mode. By contrast, the pull of tradition moves most often in the direction of withdrawal or non-interventionism. Such withdrawal is manifest in the biographies of certain writers – for example, in the splendid isolation of Croce during the years of the Fascist dictatorship, when he was tolerated by the régime in part precisely because he withdrew from the battlegrounds of explicit ideological and political debate. But symptoms of withdrawal are also amply evident within literary texts themselves, as we will see in the following section. In all that follows, however, there is no escaping the schizophrenia of literature's relationship to modernity and tradition: even here, the two constantly intermingle and overlap.

2.2. Escape from modernity

2.2.1. Landscape, childhood, memory

The rural landscape, with its sense of rootedness and sheer beauty, has been a constant in Italy's self-representations. In modern times, the countryside has, if anything, taken on even more powerful symbolic resonance, as Italy shifted from an agrarian to an urban society. Perhaps *the* key experience of modernity for millions of Italians was the wrench of migration (or emigration) away from rural homes. Literature was one means of preserving the rural landscape in the collective memory in some way, against the forces of change. Literary landscape was both a real and a symbolic space, rich with the resonances of memory and return, of mourned lost worlds. Landscape was portrayed as an idealised locus of child-hood, authenticity and innocence, in tune with the impulses and temporal rhythms of nature rather than culture and history.

The single most influential writer to elaborate such a vision was Cesare Pavese. In many of his greatest works (e.g. *La casa in collina*, 'The House on the Hill', 1948; *La luna e i falò*, 'The Moon and the Bonfires', 1950), the landscape of the Langhe hills near Turin connoted a somehow pre-civilised violence, sensuality and imme-diacy. These works tapped into a mythical consciousness of the countryside as cyclical, feminine, simultaneously destructive and regenerative. The Langhe were therefore a site of escape from the modern for Pavese, but not exclusively in an 'escapist' fashion, since they also offered a perspective on and even a critique of the modern world. Thus Corrado, the hero of *La casa in collina*, first instinctively tries to use the hills as a refuge from the modern world (i.e. the war), but over the course of the novel gains insight into the nature of violence and destruction in war from those very hills.

Two further examples (of many which could be chosen), both from the middle decades of the century, illustrate the bond between landscape, childhood, memory, and the escape from the modern.

In Vittorini's *Conversazione in Sicilia* ('Conversation in Sicily', 1941), the protagonist Silvestro is mired in the 'ennui' and grey indifference of life in the city of Milan (which many have read as a veiled political allegory indicating a weariness with his and his generation's passive acquiescence to the Fascist régime). He departs on a whim for his native Sicilian village, where he will be nudged back towards a sensual and sexual (and political) vitality, all evoked in a highly lyrical, hypnotically rhythmical (Faulkner-like) prose. In the following passage, Silvestro's mother is the channel back to the lost senses of childhood, to authenticity and innocence (the herring, the mother's face, the stick to beat Silvestro with, the sun, the cold), all made 'doubly real' through memory and return:

[Mia madre si] rialzò con l'aringa in mano, tenendola verso la coda, ed esaminandola, da una parte, dall'altra; e io vidi, nell'odore dell'aringa, la sua faccia senza nulla di quando era stata una faccia giovane, come io ora ricordavo che'era stata, e con l'età che faceva un di piú su di essa. Era questo mia madre; il ricordo di quella che era stata quindici anni prima, vent'anni prima quando ci aspettava al salto dal treno merci, giovane e terribile, col legno in mano; il ricordo, e l'età di tutta la lontananza, l'in piú di ora, insomma due volte reale. [...] E questo era ogni cosa, il ricordo e l'in piú di ora, il sole, il freddo, il braciere di rame in mezzo alla cucina, e l'acquisito nella mia coscienza di quel punto del mondo dove mi trovavo; ogni cosa era questo, reale due volte.

(My mother stood up with the herring in her hand, holding it by the tail, examining it, on one side, then the other; and I saw, in the smell of the herring, her face which had nothing of when it had been a young face, as I was remembering now that it had been, and with her age which gave it something extra on top of that. This was my mother; the memory of what she had been fifteen years before, twenty years before when she waited for us at the goods train stop, young and terrifying, holding a stick; the memory and the age of all that was far off, the extra of now, so all doubly real. [...] And everything was like this, the memory of it and the extra of the here and now, the sun, the cold, the copper brazier in the middle of the kitchen, and the acceptance within me of that point in the world where I now was; everything was like this, doubly real.)

The revelatory return to the mother's hearth is also part of a process of consciousness-raising, a preliminary to an engagement with the modern world, as the anti-Fascist dimension of the novel suggests. *After* the end of the novel, Silvestro is left on a path (whose direction the reader can only guess at) towards maturity and self-defining action.

The second example, Elsa Morante's extraordinary novel *L'isola di Arturo* ('Arthur's Island', 1957), is a fabulous evocation of a childhood world not open to return. The island of Procida where Arturo spends his childhood encapsulates in the purest form the imaginary realm of childhood and innocence bonded to a natural landscape. Tapping into the archetypal power of fable and myth (with psychoanalytical echoes), Morante creates a magical world apart, in which the innocence of the child is bound up with a sort of polymorphous sexuality: Arturo worships his father, whose sexuality shifts as the novel progresses, falls in love with his step-mother, dreams of his dead mother, and all the while lives in suggestive harmony with the island itself, the sea, the castle, the village, the rocks and the beach. Every excursion is transformed by Arturo's imagination into an heroic adventure:

Siamo a Roncisvalle, e d'un tratto, sulla spianata, irromperà Orlando col suo corno. Siamo alle Termopoli, e dietro le rocce si nascondono i cavalieri persiani, coi loro berretti puntuti [...] Era un torneo famoso. Lassú ci aspettava un traguardo acclamante, e tutti i *trenta milioni di dèi!*

(We're at Roncevaux and suddenly, out on the plane, Roland erupts into view blowing his horn. We're at Thermopolis, and behind the rock the Persian knights are hiding, with their pointed helmets [...] It was a famous tournament. Up there, a celebrated victory awaited us, together with all *30 million gods!*)

This world, which Arturo believes is wholly subject to his rule, is gradually taken away from him, until he leaves the island behind at the end, thrust into the world of adulthood and loss.

2.2.2. *Religion, myth, transcendence*

Beneath the surface of the literature of landscape lies another powerful resource for evading the transient modern world. Both Pavese's eternally repeated cycles of nature and Morante's universal archetypes of childhood share a sense of searching for deeper patterns, for 'truer' connections to life than the shifting sands of today's reality could ever allow. They point us towards a literature which 'rises above' contingency and reaches for transcendence.

The search for transcendence takes many forms, in literature as in the wider culture. Inevitably for a country in which the cultural and political power of the Catholic Church has remained strong even through a century of secularisation, it manifests itself often in Christian or Christianising literature. The culture of Christianity, its images, rituals and idioms, are constant presences in modern Italian literature. So pervasive are they, they can be adapted to the most secular of causes, as in Pasolini's both highly politicised and deeply spiritual film of Matthew's Gospel (*Il vangelo secondo Matteo*, 'The Gospel According to Matthew', 1964). Their power as myth is also available to aid self-exploration of an intensely personal kind, as Pasolini again shows in his 1949 poem, 'La Crocifissione' ('The Crucifixion', from *L'usignolo della chiesa cattolica*, 'The Nightingale of the Catholic Church'), in which his own agonies of exclusion (for his homosexuality and non-conformism) are imaged in the figure of Christ on the Cross:

> Bisogna esporsi (questo insegna
> il povero Cristo inchiodato?),
> la chiarezza del cuore è degna
> di ogni scherno, di ogni peccato
> di ogni più nuda passione ...
> (questo vuol dire il Crocifisso? [...]

(We must throw ourselves open (is this what/ poor Christ nailed up
on the cross has to teach us?)/ clarity of heart is worth/ every act of
derision, every sin/ every barest passion .../ (is this what Christ
crucified means?) [...])

Pasolini is here beginning to build that paradoxical hybrid of
Marxism, Freudianism and Christianity which would dominate
his mature work. In each of these grand discourses he identified
an ideological component but also an aura of transcendence or
mystery.

Broader dimensions of transcendence, beyond the resources of
Christianity, were also at work in the literature of the century. We
can look at two examples from opposite ends of the century: first
the metaphysical war poetry of Giuseppe Ungaretti; and secondly,
the mythical storytelling of Roberto Calasso.

Ungaretti's poetry of the First World War is contained in his first
collection of verse, *L'allegria* ('Joy', built up between 1916 and
1931). *L'allegria* taps into the mysteries of the universe in a paganis-
tic, metaphysical mode, finding the depths and essence of being in
scraps of desolate battlefields and strange personal rituals. Perhaps
the most famous example is the (for him unusually) long 1916 poem
'I fiumi' ('Rivers'), in which he performs a sort of pagan baptism on
himself, cleansing his war-weary body in the river Isonzo at the
Italian-Austrian front. The poem begins as follows:

> Mi tengo a quest'albero mutilato
> abbandonato in questa dolina
> che ha il languore
> di un circo
> prima o dopo lo spettacolo
> e guardo
> il passaggio quieto
> delle nuvole sulla luna
>
> Stamani mi sono disteso
> in un'urna d'acqua

e come una reliquia
ho riposato

L'Isonzo scorrendo
mi levigava
come un suo sasso

Ho tirato su
le mie quattr'ossa
e me ne sono andato
come un acrobata
sull'acqua

Mi sono accoccolato
vicino ai miei panni
sudici di guerra
e come un beduino
mi sono chinato a ricevere
il sole

Questo è l'Isonzo
e qui meglio
mi sono riconosciuto
una docile fibra
dell'universo […]

(I cling to this maimed tree/ abandoned in this gully/ listless like/ a circus/ before or after the show/ and I watch/ the quiet passing/ of the clouds over the moon// This morning I lay down/ in an urn of water/ and like a relic/ I rested// The flowing Isonzo/ polished me/ like one of its rocks// I pulled up/ my bag of bones/ and I went on my way/ like an acrobat/ over the water// I huddled up/ near to my clothes/ with their war filth/ and like a Bedouin/ I bowed to receive/ the sun// This is the Isonzo/ and here above all/ I have seen myself as/ a docile fibre/ of the universe […])

'I fiumi' is packed with images evoking transcendence: the circus, the nightscape, the relic, the Bedouin ritual, the act of purification which seems to stand for a sort of death and rebirth. Indeed, an intimation of mortality is often a key element of the transcendent mode of writing (Ungaretti's poetry is sometimes labelled Orphic, after Orpheus, the poet who journeyed to the underworld). All this leads to the extraordinary moment of harmony between self and universe at the end of the extract, the epiphany of this eclectic, intuitive spirituality.

Transcendence does not always imply spirituality, however. Literature itself – or its antecedents, myth, song and storytelling – can also be raised to a timeless, sublime plane. In Pavese, there are strong moves in this direction in his anthropological and Jungian notions of universal, archetypal myths (*Dialoghi con Leucò*, 'Dialogues with Leucò', 1947). Late in the century, Roberto Calasso, a formidably erudite writer and cultural operator, launched a grand project of philosophical rejection of modernity in his meditation *La rovina di Kasch* (1983). This was followed by his reworking of Ancient Greek myth cycles, *Le nozze di Cadmo e di Armonia* ('The Marriage of Cadmus and Harmony', 1988), which took up Italy's imposing classical tradition as a haunting, transcendent web of stories, suspended in time: as the book's epigraph from Sallust puts it, 'These things never were, but are always'. For Calasso, literature itself is now the apt vessel not only for stories of the gods (from Greece, but also from Indian cultures, as in his later book *Ka*, 'Ka', 1996): it is the only residue of the eternal presence of the gods and their myths. Only literature can 'far sfuggire gli dèi alla clinica universale e reimmetterli nel mondo' (allow the gods to escape from the universal sick-bed and reinsert them into the world, *La letteratura e gli dèi*, 'Literature and the Gods', 2001).

2.2.3. History

A further alternative dimension to the modern world lies in the past: not only the intimate, remembered past of childhood (see above), but also the broader canvas of history.

Historical narrative – and, in particular, the genre of the 'historical novel', in which recorded events and people from history are carefully intermingled with fictional events and characters in a single, shaped narrative – has been an influential and also problematic presence in modern Italian literature. The principal reason for this is the shadow cast by one book: Alessandro Manzoni's great historical novel *I promessi sposi* ('The Betrothed', 1840). Manzoni set his novel in seventeenth-century Lombardy, and packed it with varied fare, including broad comedy and intense tragedy, love and death, confession and retribution, power, corruption and oppression, famine, riots, war and plague. The novel went well beyond these vivid ingredients, however. Manzoni was as much interested in using the past as a path to explore difficult moral and political issues, both universal and of his contemporary, nineteenth-century world. The historical novel has consistently proved hybrid in this sense, split between the detailed reconstruction of a past world as an end in its own right, as a literary and historical exercise; and the prospective use of the past to bridge forward to the present, by way of analogy, allegory, continuity or contrast. Manzoni felt the split so keenly, he eventually rejected the genre he had used so successfully.

The ambiguities of history in literature remain apparent into the twentieth century. Competing forces worked against the historical novel in the early decades of the century: it was anathema to the lyricist and idealist trends in literary prose of the period (although it had a certain niche in more popular narrative); in the middle of the century, it went against the engaged, contemporary ethic of the Neo-Realists. From the 1950s onwards, however, the historical novel entered a period of revival.

The tension with the Neo-Realists came to a head in the mid-1950s, when two of the key practitioners of Neo-Realism – novelist Vasco Pratolini and filmmaker Luchino Visconti – turned their back on contemporary subject-matter in favour of the colourful historical canvas of the nineteenth century. Pratolini's *Metello* ('Metello') and Luchino Visconti's *Senso* ('Sense') (both 1955; treating, respectively, the working-class movements of 1890s Florence and the Risorgimento politics of 1860s Venice) were accused of, precisely, betraying engaged literature and indulging in the merely escapist pleasures of history. Others defended their works as critiques of Italian unification and thus of the origins of the contradictions of present-day Italy.

A third former Neo-Realist, Italo Calvino, was in those same years writing *Il barone rampante* ('The Baron in the Trees', 1957), an extraordinary work which was part historical novel (set in the eighteenth century, with a cast of real and fictional characters), part fable or fantasy (about a boy who lives up in the trees), and part allegorical reflection on the very issues of engagement, evasion, history and responsibility (can one 'live in the trees' and also engage with the world?) under intense scrutiny in those years.

The real turning point in the fortunes of the historical novel, however, came with the 1958 (posthumous) publication of Lampedusa's *Il gattopardo*, often cited as the first literary bestseller in Italy (and famously filmed by Visconti in 1963). Lampedusa's novel is a classical instance of the historical novel in form, written out of an explicit rejection of the meagre modern world and a nostalgia for the grandeur of a lost, aristocratic past (that of the author's own ancestry). Like *Metello* or *Senso*, it presents an historical analysis of the failures and hypocrisies of the Risorgimento, but it also displays a deeper scepticism about the very notion of historical change itself, about man's capacity to alter events or the shape of human society. The hero, Prince Salina, views the apparently momentous surface changes going on around him from the exquisitely supra-historical perspective of his ancient family lineage, his fascination with astronomy and with death. From there all change is illusory: 'tutto sarà lo stesso mentre tutto sarà cambiato' (everything will remain the same as everything changes). The novel's feel for the macrocosmic rhythms of history and nature brings it close to the mythical and transcendent literature discussed earlier. A historical novel sceptical about history, *Il gattopardo* is therefore doubly detached from the literature of intervention and from modernity.

Lampedusa's scepticism about history is replayed in a 'postmodern' key in a later bestseller, Umberto Eco's *Il nome della rosa* ('The Name of the Rose', 1980). In Eco's hands, the historical elements of the historical novel − here, a thirteenth-century monastery and theological debates on heresy − are transformed into a web of texts, clues and citations, a patchwork in which Aquinas talks like Wittgenstein, a theologian acts like Sherlock Holmes (and so on). In this swirl of textualities and codes, there is no single past to offer a perspective on the present. What remains is the pleasure of the genres on display, the intellectual games and a number of philosophical notions floated along the way.

Pitched somewhere between Manzoni and Eco, a further form of historical narrative shows awareness both of the complexities of history as a form of textuality − especially in its use of documents and sources − and an engagement with moral and political issues of substance which bridge between past and present. Leonardo Sciascia, in works both fictional (*Il consiglio d'Egitto*, 'The Council of Egypt', 1973) and factual (*Morte dell'Inquisitore*, 'Death of the Inquisitor', 1964), uses historical documents and records with great subtlety to lead on to reflections on his perennial 'political' concerns of justice, deception and the workings of power and authority. Sciascia would later apply some of these techniques of archival enquiry to a meditation on a contemporary event, the kidnap and murder of the Christian Democrat leader Aldo Moro (*L'affaire Moro*, 'The Moro Affair', 1978).

Finally, certain historical novels from the 1960s onwards attempted a much more explicitly anti-escapist, engaged use of history, pushing the possibilities of analogy with and critique of the present through the eyes of the past. A good example of this is the gendered revision of history in a line of novels by women in the last quarter of the century. Elsa Morante's 1974 work, *La storia* ('History'), opened up new perspectives on very recent history − the Second World War − by writing about it in the manner of an historical novel, mixing public history (in the form of brief, semi-serious historical summaries of the events of the war) with the fictional and private (the story of a mother and her son born of a rape by a Nazi soldier in Rome). Similar issues emerge in Dacia Maraini's 1990 novel *La lunga vita di Marianna Ucrìa* ('The Long Life of Marianna Ucrìa'), whose eighteenth-century setting veils Maraini's interest in contemporary issues such as the subordination, silencing and resistance of women (the heroine is left deaf and dumb, literally silent, following a childhood rape).

2.2.4. Literary tradition

In literature, tradition persists most insistently in the form of the *literary* tradition itself. Authors work in relation to their predecessors in the literary canon, through what the American critic Harold Bloom famously labelled 'the anxiety of influence'. They pick up on and challenge traditional literary forms, develop their style in relation to received conventions of beauty, elegance and literariness (or their contravention). Indeed, one could argue that the very notion of literature only makes sense as long as writers are conscious of a literary tradition that they both absorb and struggle against. The lack of any such consciousness amongst some young writers of the end of the century – who proved more interested in MTV than medieval poetry – was, therefore, the cause of laments over the death of literature. And one could argue further that, in the specific case of Italy, the weight of tradition was particularly deeply felt (at least until the latter part of the twentieth century). The reasons for this are ones I have touched on before, but they are worth reiterating here.

First, the legacy of Renaissance humanism – that is, the bedrock devotion of the Renaissance to the recovery and study of the classical tradition – continued to be felt powerfully in the education of the literary élite in the twentieth century, reinforced by the Fascist education reforms of 1923, which established the 'liceo classico', a secondary school system with strong emphasis on the study of Latin and Greek as the highest possible attainment of the young student. Not the least effect of this focus on classics was the continuing primacy of an elaborate, Latinate syntax in literary prose style (indeed in all formal, public arenas), which detached literary Italian from everyday usage of the language.

The Renaissance legacy showed through not only in the language and in a humanistic respect for the classics, but also in a general sense of the authority of the past. Thus, sixteenth-century thinkers imitated their own awe of the classics by building up a canon of vernacular writers also – Dante, Petrarch, Boccaccio – and this created a mindset in which these three (the so-called 'tre corone' or 'three crowns') and other so-called 'grandi' (great writers) cast long shadows forward.

Furthermore, the image of Italy itself as a storeroom of great cultural heritage (both without and within Italy), and the identification of the nation as formed within the sphere of culture (especially before unification), meant that the prestige and pride of Italy was continually bound up with past traditions, literary and otherwise.

These forces pushed much literature towards the literary tradition, over and above contact with the world that surrounded it. There is long-term evidence of this in the extraordinary, continued flourishing of lyric poetry in twentieth-century Italy (and a parallel resistance to the novel, at least in the first half of the century), where the Petrarchan tradition and its legacy flourished even in the loosest, free-form verse (as epitomised by Ungaretti). It is there also in the so-called 'ritorno all'ordine' (return to order) of 1920s literature (evident in Ungaretti's second major collection of verse, *Sentimento del tempo*, 'Feeling of Time', 1933); and in the baroque language of 'prosa d'arte' and later writers, as noted in our discussion of language in Chapter 1.

But as with other categories examined in this chapter, the valency which equates literariness with tradition and the evasion of the modern, can be inverted at times, in unpredictable and striking ways. To write a Petrarchan sonnet is hardly to penetrate to the heart of modernity; however, done with the sophisticated wordplay and irony of Andrea Zanzotto, it can be turned comically to evoke an everyday torment, the dentist: his 'Sonetto degli interminabili lavori dentarii' ('Sonnet on Interminable Dental Work') (*Il Galateo in bosco*, 'The Galateo in the Woods', 1978) laments the passing of his dying teeth, the long days and years of their struggle, the pain of their extraction, until he sees himself as no more than an 'incerta collana/ di segni-morsi da pròtesi inferti' (an uncertain garland / of bite-signs inflicted by prostheses). Here, Zanzotto strips away the aura of the sonnet – typically a vehicle for love poetry – but his language is still highly wrought, a parody of more than one arcane literary idiom. As with Eco's game-playing with history, this approaches the realm of the postmodern, in which the elements of tradition and the canon – citation, homage, self-conscious literariness – are turned into a reflection of a hypermodernity in which timelines and hierarchies of cultural value are confused and fragmented.

It is, of course, also important to note that the uses of literary influence are not always preciously introverted: the tradition remains a potent source for a literature 'politically' engaged with modernity, in some hands at least. And this has perhaps especially been true of the influence of Dante on twentieth-century literature. Vittorini's *Conversazione in Sicilia*, discussed above, uses several Dantesque elements to forge its style, structure and political message (the three-day descent into another world; the guided encounter with shady figures with stories to tell, etc.). Pasolini attempted a full-scale modern version of the *Inferno*, in *La divina mimesis* ('Divine Mimesis', 1975) and later *Petrolio* ('Oil', 1992), as a way of damning the new consumer society he saw around him. And Primo Levi famously drew richly on Dante, in *Se questo è un uomo* ('If This is a Man', 1947) and elsewhere, to shape his account of one of the key sites of modernity, Auschwitz (see Chapter 7.4).

*

As we have seen, motifs of withdrawal and tradition often invert to engage in interesting ways with modernity, just as later we will see strenuous efforts to be modern proving, in practice, rather staid and retrograde. But these inversions should not divert us from the underlying point of this chapter, that is the remarkable persistence of an idea of literature as somehow beyond the concerns of the changing world, as in some way pure, absolute, 'not for now but for all time'. In conclusion, it is worth linking this idea of literature in general terms to the immensely influential philosopher, historian and critic, Benedetto Croce. Croce argued for an idealist conception of history as a progression of ideas (such as freedom) rather than a sequence of recorded dates and events. And he located literature in lyrical or essential moments of 'poesia' (poetry) which tapped into such ideas, moments to be isolated from the structures of information, explanation or concept which surrounded them in a given work. These notions militated powerfully for a pure, non-interventionist sense of what literature should strive to be. And Croce's weighty authority in all things philosophical and literary for at least the first two-thirds of the twentieth century in Italy can hardly be overstated. Nevertheless, as the following chapters will show, the field of literature could never wholly isolate itself from the progress of modernity in the wider world.

Selected reading

Harold Bloom, *The Anxiety of Influence: A Theory of Poetry* (New York: Oxford University Press, 1973). Bloom's influential 'Oedipal' theory of how writers struggle with the literary tradition (see section 2.2.4 above).

Cristina Della Coletta, *Plotting the Past: Metamorphoses of Historical Narrative in Modern Italian Fiction* (West Lafayette, IN: Purdue UP, 1996). On the modern historical novel (2.2.3).

Luciano De Maria (ed.), *Per conoscere Marinetti e il futurismo* (Milan: Mondadori, 1981). The richest anthology of Futurist manifestos and creative writings (2.1).

Umberto Eco, *Apocalittici e integrati* (Milan: Bompiani, 1964); title essay in English in *Apocalypse Postponed* (London: BFI, 1994) (2.1).

John Gatt-Rutter, *Writers and Politics in Modern Italy* (London: Hodder & Stoughton, 1978) (2.1).

Lucia Re, *Calvino and the Age of Neorealism* (Stanford: Stanford University Press, 1990). The first two chapters of this study of Calvino's early work offer an excellent analysis of Neo-Realist narrative (2.1).

Doug Thompson, *Cesare Pavese* (Cambridge: Cambridge University Press, 1982) (2.2.1).

Raymond Williams, *Keywords. A Vocabulary of Culture and Society* (London: Fontana, 1976). See, among others, entries on 'modern', 'nature', 'city', 'country' (2.1).

3

Modern Worlds

Modernity altered the very contours of the world we live in. It brought with it new spaces to inhabit, new ways of moving in the world, and new worlds to imagine. A perception of the world made anew exploded onto the Italian cultural scene with the launch of the Futurist movement in 1909: as one of their manifesto declarations put it, 'time and space died yesterday: we are already living in the Absolute'. From this moment on, the humanist and isolationist tendencies of literature came under sustained challenge from at least a part of the literary field, keen to represent the spaces and dynamics of the modern world. This chapter explores four of these new spaces or dynamics, as seen through literature.

3.1. The city

The city has been a central feature of Italy's history since well before the twentieth century. The medieval city-states of Central and Northern Italy were, famously, the motors behind the wealth, power and flourishing culture which created the Italian Renaissance. And with the city-states came a powerful ideal of civic culture, together with the often catastrophic failure to live up to that ideal (as fiercely denounced by Dante in the *Commedia*, with its elaborate imagery of the city, human and divine). While the Italian city was by no means a twentieth-century invention, then, it certainly altered radically with the twentieth century. An urban model born in nineteenth-century, industrial-revolution Northern Europe began to emerge in Italy also; agrarian society entered a period of decline, and mass urbanisation emerged as the dominant thread of social change of the new century. The modern city was quite alien to the (apparently) contained, ordered, hierarchical, classically inspired city-state. It was rather imagined and experienced as the city of the crowd, of work, of extremes of poverty and wealth, of new forms of surveillance and policing; and, at the same time, as a vital space, open to opportunity, personal and social transformation and the levelling out of hierarchy. It was a space of danger, struggle and a new form of heroism, as charted in the nineteenth-century European novel by figures such as Balzac, Hugo and Dickens, among many others. In Italy, the nineteenth century did not see the emergence of a strong tradition of this kind of novel, but from the early twentieth century, a body of narrative reflecting the enthusiasm and anxiety bred by the modern city began to emerge (both in the novel and, as we will see, in the visual narrative of cinema).

We can make three approaches to the vast field of representations of the modern city. First of all, we can pick out one key, recurrent narrative scene, which seems to encapsulate the processes and meanings of urbanisation in modern Italy: the scene of first arrival in the city. In all its variations, the scene of arrival acts as a marker of the strangeness and newness of the city, and also of that dual affect of hope and fear engendered by modernity. In sociological terms, it resonates with the experience of migration or emigration shared by millions of Italians through the century. A particularly haunting image of this is found in the opening sequence of Visconti's 1960 film, *Rocco e i suoi fratelli* ('Rocco and His Brothers'), in which a huddled family arrive by train from the deep rural South, dwarfed by Milan's monstrous, expressionistically lit 'Stazione centrale', as a plaintive Southern ballad plays on the soundtrack. The same 'Stazione centrale' was the subject of an extraordinary piece of night-time narrative-cum-reportage by Anna Maria Ortese, in 'Una notte nella stazione' ('A Night at the Station' in *Silenzio a Milano*, 'Silence in Milan', 1958).

Arrival in the city often also marks a formative moment in a trajectory towards becoming an artist and/or an adult, in any number of works rooted in autobiography. Federico Fellini, for example, told and retold the story of his departure from the sleepy town of Rimini for the bright lights of Rome (e.g. *I vitelloni*, 'The Layabouts', 1953; *Fellini Roma*, 1972). Sibilla Aleramo's proto-feminist narrative of liberation, *Una donna* (1906), told of her traumatic break with her husband and young son enacted in her move from the provinces to Rome. Conversely, in a powerful novel from the end of the century by Elena Ferrante, *L'amore molesto* ('Troublesome Love', 1992) (later filmed by Mario Martone), arrival in the city is now experienced as a scene of return, as the protagonist uneasily rediscovers the chaotic and sexually ambivalent Naples of her childhood and so comes to terms with her mother's death and repressed memories of trauma.

The scene of arrival is also used as a marker of a sociological and conceptual transformation. Luigi Pirandello's experimental novel, *Il fu Mattia Pascal* ('The Late Mattia Pascal', 1904) – one of the best candidates available for a text to mark the start of twentieth-century Italian literature – contains a moment of arrival in Rome to rival (and, in some sense, to parody) those of the nineteenth-century novelists, when Mattia, shorn of his identity and dreaming of an entirely new existence, resolves nervily that Rome is the place to go. The novel's ninth chapter ends: 'Bisognava ch'io vincessi ogni ritegno, prendessi a ogni costo una risoluzione. Io, insomma dovevo vivere, vivere, vivere' (I had to conquer all restraint, take action at all costs. In short, I had to live, to live, to live); and the tenth chapter opens as follows:

Pochi giorni dopo ero a Roma, per prendervi dimora.
    Perché a Roma e non altrove? [...] Scelsi allora Roma, prima di tutto perché mi piacque sopra ogni altra città, e poi perché mi parve piú adatta a ospitar con indifferenza, tra tanti forestieri, un forestiere come me.

(A few days later I was in Rome, looking for lodgings.
    Why Rome and not somewhere else? [...] I chose Rome first of all because it was my favourite of all cities, and then because I

thought it would be the most likely place to welcome with indifference a stranger like myself, in the midst of so many other strangers.)

Here, the city is a mix of sociological reality – a place of indifference where the individual can merge anonymously into the crowd, and of what would now be called 'multicultural' identity where outsiders or foreigners are the norm – and a conceptual space for identity formation, where the city stands for the ecstatic possibility ('vivere, vivere, vivere'), and ultimately, as the novel shows, the failure of self-reinvention.

Our second approach to the city in literature looks at the city architectonically, as construction and as constructed space. Futurism made a major, if unrealised, contribution to architectural modernism through the work of Antonio Sant'Elia, creator of a series of inspiring and influential modernist drawings of futuristic urban spaces, and of the 1914 manifesto 'L'architettura futurista' ('Futurist Architecture'), before his death at the front in 1916. A strongly modernist conception of space fed into much Fascist architecture, realised in a large number of urban building projects, from state buildings to entire towns, where urban space was explicitly choreographed with a view to the glorification of the state, the party, the Duce and the subsuming of the individual within these. The same relation – of the individual to the built environment – recurs in postwar literature, often now focused on the unplanned, often illegal urban sprawl of Italian cities. Pasolini's semi-slum peripheries, the 'borgate' (e.g. *Ragazzi di vita*, 1955), are good examples: on the edge of Rome and other cities, after the war, the urban poor clustered in makeshift dwellings, often within yards of ancient Roman ruins and humming building sites. For Pasolini, the very spaces of the 'borgate', the architecture of gaps, fragments and ruins, opening up deep spaces of poverty but also freedom, stood symbolically for the marginalised and unfettered humanity which inhabited them. Moving up the social scale, Calvino's *La speculazione edilizia* ('Illegal Construction', 1963) charted the illegal sprawl in one small northern city, around which local politics and personal narratives intertwine.

Perhaps the key figure to show how the architecture and the spaces of the city conditioned the modern individual was the filmmaker Michelangelo Antonioni. In his 1962 film, *L'eclisse* ('The Eclipse'), the imposing modern architecture of Rome, from the Stock Exchange to Mussolini's high-modernist city-extension EUR, comes to dominate the film to such an extent that the flimsy affairs of human emotion are shut out in the final few minutes of the film. A street corner in EUR, with its geometric lines and random, banal passing events, is shown alone, two lovers having failed to meet there as planned.

Our third and final take on the city picks up on Antonioni's geometric, dehumanised vision of the modern city, looking at it as idea or concept, rather than place; as an abstract, imaginary and, on occasion, magic and transformatory space. In this guise, the city becomes a reinvention of some of the most ancient archetypes of myth and narrative, such as the labyrinth or the dark wood, and also a vessel of the most modern (and even postmodern) confusions and multiplications of boundaries and meanings. The tangled webs of Carlo Emilio Gadda's cities, such as the Rome of *Quer pasticciaccio brutto de via Merulana* ('That Awful Mess on Via Merulana', 1957), have much of this quality, as do the dynamic, electric cities of the Futurist collage poems or paintings. But the most extraordinary expression of this imaginary city in twentieth-century Italian literature is undoubtedly Calvino's 1972 work *Le città invisibili*, in which Marco Polo relates to his Emperor Kublai Khan his travels to the beguiling cities of the Khan's empire, each one stranger and more elusive than the last. Here is the approach (another stranger arriving in a city) to one of them, Zoe, a city of shimmering multiplicities:

L'uomo che viaggia e non conosce ancora la città che lo aspetta lungo la strada, si domanda come sarà la reggia, la caserma, il mulino, il teatro, il bazar. In ogni città dell'impero ogni edificio è differente e disposto in un diverso ordine: ma appena il forestiero arriva alla città sconosciuta e getta lo sguardo in mezzo a quella pigna di pagode e abbaini e fienili, seguendo il ghirigoro di canali orti immondezzai, subito distingue quali sono i palazzi dei principi, quali i templi dei grandi sacerdoti, la locanda, la prigione, la suburra. Cosí – dice qualcuno – si conferma l'ipotesi che ogni uomo porta nella mente una città fatta soltanto di differenza, una città senza figure e senza forma, e le città particolari la riempiono.

Non cosí a Zoe. In ogni luogo di questa città si potrebbe volta a volta dormire, fabbricare arnesi, cucinare, accumulare monete d'oro, svestirsi, regnare, vendere, interrogare oracoli. Qualsiasi tetto a piramide potrebbe coprire tanto il lazzaretto dei lebbrosi quanto le terme delle odalische. Il viaggiatore gira gira e non ha che dubbi: [...] la città di Zoe è il luogo dell'esistenza indivisibile.

(A traveller who does not yet know the city that awaits him further along the road wonders what the royal palace, the barracks, the mill, the theatre, the bazaar will be like. In every city of the empire, every building is different and set out in a different order: but as soon as the stranger reaches the unknown city and looks around at the cluster of pagodas and lofts and barns, following the gurgling of canals, orchards, rubbish tips, he can see at once which buildings are the princes' palaces, which the temples of the high priest, the inn, the prison, the slum. So confirming – some might say – the theory that every man carries within him a city made only of differences, a city without figures or shapes, which each individual city merely fills out.

But Zoe is different. In every part of this city, you could at one time or another sleep, make tools, cook, gather gold coins, undress, rule, sell, interrogate oracles. Any pointed roof could hide the leper colony or the odalisque's baths. The traveller walks on and on but is assailed only by doubt. [...] Zoe is the city of indivisible existence.)

All the cities of *Le città invisibili* tease out some of the conceptual complexities of modernity (and/or postmodernity) through the magical redescription of city spaces.

3.2. Machines

The driving force behind industrial modernisation and the changes in habitat and way of life brought about by modernity has been technology, informed by modern science. A list of the momentous technological innovations which began dramatically to change lives around the turn of the twentieth century is easily compiled: the engineering of skyscrapers, the engine for the automobile and the aeroplane, the moving-image camera, the gas and electricity to light up cities, and so on. And the century which followed would see these inventions and innovations multiply, from radio and television, to nuclear weapons, the pill and space travel, all the way to the internet, mobile phones and biogenetics.

Literature, and the humanities in general, proved deeply reluctant to engage with this fundamental modern form of knowledge (science) and its applications (technology), as famously captured in C.P. Snow's portrait of 'The Two Cultures', one humanistic and one scientific, mutually deaf if not hostile to each other's concerns. Italian literary culture, humanistic in origin and generally hostile to the nineteenth-century's 'positivist' interest in observable data, facts and mechanisms, shared this suspicion of science. Nevertheless, the century's literature also threw up a cluster of important writers who, on the contrary, were deeply and diversely engaged with science and technology, picking up on a legacy of cross-disciplinary knowledge left by immense, canonical figures such as Dante, Leonardo da Vinci, Galileo and others. This minor modern canon starts, inevitably, with the Futurists, who explicitly proposed a 'mechanics' of art, in which art is produced not by aesthetics but by the movement, rotation, construction, decomposition and interpenetration of 'plastic' matter; and goes on to include, among others, Carlo Emilio Gadda (an engineer by training), Italo Calvino (son of botanists), and the chemist Primo Levi.

We can follow three different paths to illustrate the web connecting science and literature in the twentieth century, each focused on a particular, emblematic machine. The first is the machine of

movement *par excellence*, which opened up the working and leisure
journeys of modern life to the masses as the century progressed: the
car. Take two literary automobiles dated, respectively, from the
early part of the century and the 1960s. In both cases, the car is a
hybrid machine, with attributes of both classical, mythical force
(the car as chariot) and of the technological modern. The first is in
Marinetti's poem 'All'Automobile di corsa' ('To the Racing Car';
first published in French in 1908), in which the car is poised
between late-Symbolist decadence (it is a god, a drug, an equine
monster, an erotic dancer and demon, explicitly echoing the nineteenth-century French poet Charles Baudelaire at the end) and
Futurist worship of the modern:

> Veemente dio d'una razza d'acciaio,
> Automobile ebbra di spazio,
> che scalpiti e fremi d'angoscia
> rodendo il morso con striduli denti ...
> Formidabile mostro giapponese,
> dagli occhi di fucina,
> nutrito di fiamma
> e d'oli minerali, avido d'orrizonti, di prede siderali...
>
> [...]
>
> Che importa, mio demone bello?
> In sono in tua balìa! ... Prendimi! ... Prendimi! ...

(Fierce god of a race of steel,/ car drunk on space,/ pawing and
trembling with fear/ champing the bit with your shrill teeth .../
Fearful Japanese monster,/ with your forged eyes/ fed by flames/
and mineral oils, greedy for far horizons, for heavenly prey ...//
What does it matter, my beautiful demon?/ I am in your power! ...
Take me! ... Take me! ...)

Marinetti's febrile celebration of the car seems somewhat excessive
now, but the attempt to fuse this modern machine with a Dionysian

rhetoric of myth and loss of self is symptomatic. Something of the same imagery – the car as chariot, as a symbol of play, freedom from responsibility, carnivalesque sexual transgression and escape from conformism and stasis – survives in the pastiche and experimentalism of Alberto Arbasino's polyphonic novels of the 1960s, *Fratelli d'Italia* ('Brothers of Italy'; first edition 1963, followed by several rewritten versions) and *Super-Eliogabalo* ('Super-Heliogabalus', 1969).

To calm and qualify these hedonistic visions of the car, we can turn to rationalists such as Italo Calvino and Primo Levi. In Calvino's 'geometrical' short story, 'L'avventura di un automobilista' ('The Adventure of a Car-Driver'; in *Gli amori difficili*, 'Difficult Loves', 1970), the car traps the characters (X, Y and Z, caught in a love 'triangle'), reducing their fraught emotional lives to the motion of bodies (cars) along a straight line (the motorway) between their hometowns A and B. Levi's short story, 'Cladonia rapida' ('Cladonia rapida', in *Storie naturali*, 'Natural Histories', 1966), worries about the interface between machines and organic matter or biology (a key anxiety of the century of science, especially at its end), by imagining the pathology of a disease of cars.

Levi's work in science-fiction offers a good link to our second line of representation of the machine in the twentieth century, the use of the machine as a way of thinking about (and telling stories about) the category of the human. A good example is Levi's playlet, 'Il sesto giorno' ('The Sixth Day', in *Storie naturali*). 'Il sesto giorno' retells the Genesis story of the six days of God's creation of Man, as a story of corporate management. Humankind is a machine/animal commissioned by an 'Executive Management Council' with certain design specifications (using his anthropological insight, Levi imagines four in particular: toolmaking capacities, language, resistance to extreme conditions, socialising tendencies). 'Il sesto giorno' demystifies and parodies both the Creation story and humankind's arrogant assumptions about its privileged place in the world; the story shows how the species was born of a botched committee job, and, as a result, is destined to harm the equilibrium of the planet Earth.

This light irony is all a far cry from the excesses of Marinetti's violent, priapic, powerlusting, primitive and modern man-as-machine, the eponymous hero of his 1909 novel, *Mafarka il futurista* ('Mafarka the Futurist').

Our third emblematic machine – after the car and humankind itself – is the greatest fantasy- and pleasure-producing machine of the century, cinema. A modern technology for art (even if, for some, a debased form of art), cinema is a key test case for the attitude of the literary culture to the modern. Early responses of writers to cinema moved between contempt and fascination. The Turinese poet of the so-called 'crepuscolare' (twilight) grouping, Guido Gozzano, was eloquently damning: 'This art ... but what am I saying: this celluloid industry: this wanton and fortunate daughter of the old woman who used to wander through our squares and markets with a block of painted canvas up on a stick showing the tearful story of Genoveffa, Rosina and the unfaithful cavalier' (1916). Nevertheless, in 1911, he had collaborated on a documentary film. Verga, d'Annunzio, Pirandello and many other contemporary writers all sold work to the cinema and all expressed more or less mild forms of disapproval. Meanwhile, this and following generations were being seduced by the pleasures of the screen. Pirandello wrote one of the earliest significant novels about cinema, *Si gira* ('Shoot', 1916), and d'Annunzio famously penned the intertitles for the great epic film *Cabiria* ('Cabiria', 1916). By the 1920s, Charlie Chaplin was a hero for intellectuals as for the masses, and the critic Giacomo Debenedetti could write in 1931 of 'the conversion of the intellectuals to the cinema'.

A similar story of ambivalence and enthusiasm runs through into the postwar era when (as noted in Chapter 1) a large number of writers worked for and wrote about the cinema. The emblematic figure here was Pasolini, who, in 1960, boldly moved from being an established literary intellectual to become one of the most original and intense of filmmakers of the 1960s and 1970s. But

perhaps even more important than the high-level individual contacts between writers and filmmaking is the extent to which
literature tapped into and expressed the magic of the screen, of the
visit to the cinema as experienced by the ordinary spectator, and
the ways in which the fantasies produced there were constitutive of
a sense of self in the modern world. Here is Francesca Sanvitale's
account, in her 1980 novel *Madre e figlia* ('Mother and Daughter'),
of the glamour of the girl-star Shirley Temple, as experienced by a
young girl, reflecting the beaming, dynamic phantasmagoria of the
screen:

> Shirley per quattro ore ballava e cantava per loro, muovendo i
> ricciolini legati da un gran fiocco di taffetà, cambiando di continuo
> vestiti: a fiori, a gale, arricciature, da giorno e da sera, grembiuli a
> quadretti e sottanelle di velluto nero, cappotti con colletti di ermel-
> lino e di coniglio, manicotti e borsette, e sotto spuntavano le gambe
> grassocce da bambina ben nutrita e in cima il sorriso birichino e le
> caratteristiche fossette che l'avevano resa cosí simpatica. [...]
>   A Shirley ne succedevano di cotte e di crude e lei risolveva le sue
> e le altrui patetiche o comiche avventure di modo che alla fine c'era
> una generale, esplosiva festa di suoni e di canti dove Shirley ballava
> e cantava con marinai, canterini, ballerine, attrici e via via, tanto da
> rimanere allegeriti e allegri per giorni interi.

(Shirley danced and sang for them for four hours, shaking her curls
about in their great taffeta ribbon, changing dresses all the time,
ones with flowers, frills, gathers, daywear or eveningwear, check
smocks, little black velvet skirts, overcoats with hare and ermine
collars, muffs and handbags, and beneath them all, her chubby
baby legs and on top her naughty smile and her special dimples
which endeared her to so many people. [...]
  Shirley got into all sorts of trouble but she would sort out her own
and others people's sad or funny adventures so that at the end, there
was a general, explosive celebration of sound and song, and Shirley
would dance and sing with sailors, choristers, ballerinas, actresses
and more. It all left you feeling light as air and happy for days on
end.)

3.3. Journeys

As the Futurists loudly declared, the essence of modernity was speed, dynamism, movement. Cities are sites of infinite, intersecting lines of movement; cars (and trains, aeroplanes, etc.) allow previously unheard-of speed; the technologies of modernity promised rapid transfer or communication from one place to another. Locomotion was the key tenor of modern life, both within local circles of individual lives, and in long-distance, global geography, and travel was one key manifestation of that locomotion. The century was, after all, one of mass travel, of the shrinking globe, of the first-hand experience of other worlds.

Literature and travel, in general and in the case of Italy in particular, intersect at several different levels. Since Homer, Virgil and Dante, since Marco Polo and Swift's Gulliver, literature has always used journeys, real and imaginary, to structure narrative and to fascinate. Italy had been a principal destination for travellers on the Grand Tour of the eighteenth century and, increasingly over the nineteenth and twentieth centuries, for the not-so-grand, common tourist. In the twentieth century, travel writing became a staple for many writers, a source of journalistic income and publications, as attested to by the string of accounts (some heavily colonialist in nature) of journeys to India (e.g. Gozzano, Moravia, Pasolini), Africa (e.g. Riccardo Bacchelli, Giovanni Comisso, Gianni Celati), Russia, China and Japan (e.g. Curzio Malaparte, Goffredo Parise, Fosco Maraini) and America (see below), to say nothing of a rich literature of travel *within* Italy (e.g. Guido Piovene's *Viaggio in Italia*, 'Journey around Italy', 1957).

By the end of the century, however, the aura of the isolated literary traveller-cum-anthropologist sending back dispatches from elsewhere, was hard to sustain. New patterns of travel had created a global network of what the French anthropologist Marc Augé has called 'non-places': airport terminals, station concourses, malls, motorway service stations, a series of sites with little connection to local cultures, where passengers drift in endless connection with other such sites, briefly pausing to experience the (at least apparently) 'real' places. Something of this condition (its vacuity, but also its postmodern pleasures) is found in Pier Vittorio Tondelli's 1985 novel *Rimini* ('Rimini'), which captures the kitsch mix of sex, music and sun of the late twentieth-century seaside tourist resort, packed with Italian and European youth.

Journeying out into a newly accessible world can amount, therefore, either to a search for the slow, the unspoiled, the premodern or to a rapid plunge into modernity. But even in the most contemporary of settings, the literary journey retains 'slower' elements, of discovery and self-discovery, of individual and shared memory, of a play between home and elsewhere, of an (often impossible) escape from static, bound, modern lives. In *Il fu Mattia Pascal*, Mattia's journeys first to Monte Carlo and then to Rome are, precisely, failed attempts to escape towards a new self and a new life. Daniele Del Giudice's enigmatic 1983 novel *Lo stadio di Wimbledon* ('Wimbledon Stadium') culminates in a low key, but strangely revelatory journey to the anonymous streets of south-west London, where traces of a mystery in Trieste's past are found. The same combination – of a questing journey and a self-consciously literary and memorial dimension – underpins perhaps the most sophisticated travelogue of the final years of the century, Claudio Magris' *Danubio* (1986). Magris traces a journey along the great river in which erudition and cultural echo come together to evoke Europe's past and problems of collective memory, but also an intense sense of the mobile evanescence of all things, natural and human. Here he is, for example, reflecting on a point in the river, near its source, where it dries up and remerges at different places at different times of the year:

Anche il Danubio, al pari di ognuno di noi, è un *Noteentiendo*, un Nonticapisco, come la figura disegnata in uno dei sedici quadri della tabella 'Las Castas', una specie di gioco dell'oca dell'amore e delle stirpi che ricordo aver visto appeso a una parete del Museo di Città del Messico. [...] La tabella vorrebbe classificare e distinguere rigorosamente – anche negli abiti – le caste, sociali e razziali, ma

finisce per esaltare involontariamente il gioco capriccioso e ribelle
di eros, il grande distruttore di ogni chiusa gerarchia sociale [...]
Quel Danubio che c'è e che non c'è, che nasce da piú parti e da piú
genitori, ci ricorda che ognuno, grazie alla molteplice e nascosta
trama cui deve la sua esistenza è un Noteentiendo.

(The Danube, like each one of us, is a *Noteentiendo*, an 'Idontunder-
standyou', like one of the sixteen figures drawn onto the 'Las Castas'
table, a sort of snakes-and-ladders game of love and ancestry that I
recall seeing hanging in the museum in Mexico City. [...] The table
is designed to classify and rigorously distinguish between social and
racial castes – even down to the clothing – but all it manages
instead, despite itself, is to celebrate the capricious and rebellious
games of Eros, the great destroyer of all closed social hierarchy [...]
The Danube, which is there and is not there, which is born in
different places, from different progenitors, reminds us that each of
us, thanks to the multiple and hidden web behind our existence, is
a Noteentiendo.)

Here Magris wanders in his mind, from the Danube riverbank to
Mexico City, from the card games and cultures of other worlds to
the multiple identities of Mitteleuropa to a general sense of the
enigma of the self. And he goes on further to show his acute
awareness that the writer too is part of this enigmatic journey,
'filling in white spaces' on a map, 'noting down the names on
stations and street corners', as the traveller moves ceaselessly on.

3.4. America

In Italy, as in so many other places in the twentieth century, one
particular 'other world' impinged more powerfully than any other
on the local culture, embodying all that was fascinating and appalling about modernity: America.

Several of the elements touched on in this chapter were perceived as American: from the modern city to modern technology,
from modern music to cinema and later television. At the same

time, in social, economic and political terms, America seemed to represent for many (especially during the years of Fascism) a new kind of society, removed from the strictures and traditions of old Europe, free and open. Even in terms of natural landscape, America was perceived (and perceived itself) as a land of immense open spaces, modern epic struggles and individual destinies forged by the land (reflected in modern epic genres such as the Western film). In this it seemed to combine the power of both modern and ancient worlds.

On top of these general myths and perceptions circulating about America, Italy's history intertwined with America's in several specific ways over the course of the century. Millions of Italian emigrants from the late nineteenth century onwards reached America and settled in Italian-American communities there, with complex links back home. Between 1943 and 1945, Americans moved from being enemies to being hailed as liberators from Fascism. After the war, Italy became a cultural and political frontline in the Cold War, and American images and cultural values were powerfully promoted, at times against the wishes of the Communist opposition and the Church or the Christian Democrat governments (all of which were, after all, culturally conservative institutions).

For all these reasons, myths and images of America, pleasures and anxieties about things American, loomed very large indeed in twentieth-century Italian culture. To gauge this, we can look at a sample of literary images of America taken from different points in the century.

It is perhaps significant to note that the richest accounts of emigrant America are to be found not in Italian literature, but in the extensive field of Italian-American literature, which lies beyond our scope here. Back in Italy, especially in the literature of the South of the first part of the century, emigrants' experiences and dreams of America register as often wrenching, strange stories of long absences, fantasies of success, and occasional failure and return. 'L'altro figlio' ('The Other Son'), a 1905 short story by

Pirandello, offers a vignette of what is left behind in the wake of emigration: for years, an illiterate mother in Sicily dictates letters to a local woman and sends them off, every time another local man emigrates, to her two emigrant sons in America, in the forlorn hope she can stay in touch with them. She has never received a reply, and it emerges that the 'scribe' has only ever written nonsense.

Similarly oblique or marginal evocations of emigration – chat about the riches to be won across the ocean, men missing from the local village, or returnees, broken and isolated by their failure to find fortune – are to be seen in corners of key texts of the rural South such as Ignazio Silone's *Fontamara* ('Fontamara', 1933), where there is a character called 'Sciarappa', from 'Shut up'; or Carlo Levi's *Cristo si è fermato a Eboli* (1945), where Levi points out that in Gagliano, his village of exile in Basilicata, there are 1,200 inhabitants, but there are over 2,000 Gaglianesi in America. And in a humorous vein, Leonardo Sciascia would evoke the obtuse communication between Sicilians and their visiting Italo-American relations in his story 'La zia d'America' ('My American Aunt', in *Gli zii di Sicilia*, 'Sicilian Uncles', 1958).

Another image of America, fed by both the power of popular culture and the raw energy of American writing, emerges in Italian culture in the 1930s. American comics, genre fiction (detective novels and other popular forms) and literary novels were popular with readers and so also with publishers, even those sympathetic to the Fascist regime such as Mondadori in Milan, who published everything from *Topolino* (Mickey Mouse) to F. Scott Fitzgerald. American films, at least until the *de facto* embargo placed on them by the Fascist regime in 1938, were by far the most popular at the box-office, and Hollywood gossip and glamour drew readers to magazines in Italy as elsewhere (the future filmmaker Cesare Zavattini famously penned a fake Hollywood gossip column for several years in the early 1930s for the magazine *Cinema illustrazione*).

In the literary field, several distinguished writers, some of them anti-Fascist exiles (e.g. Gaetano Salvemini), travelled to America at this time and published accounts of their impressions. Some were positively excited by the energy and modernity of the place (e.g. Mario Soldati, *America primo amore*, 'America First Love', 1935) while others came away struck by the materialism and violence of American society (e.g. Emilio Cecchi, *America amara*, 'Bitter America', 1939). All, however, displayed an ambivalent mix of attraction and repulsion.

More significant still was the emergence in the 1930s of a group of future anti-Fascist writers (Cesare Pavese, Elio Vittorini, and others), who were powerfully drawn to American literature. Pavese's translation of Melville's classic *Moby Dick* was a treasured possession for many of his generation (as Primo Levi recalls in his 1975 memoir, *Il sistema periodico*, 'The Periodic Table'), and he and others wrote essays on and translated a string of contemporary American writers, from Steinbeck to Faulkner to Dos Passos to Hemingway, on occasion running into trouble with Fascist censors (as in the case of the anthology edited by Vittorini in 1941, *Americana*). They went on to use this literature as a model for their own work, evoking the raw, lyrical intensity of contemporary real lives and landscapes, which they saw as a way out of the stultifying preciousness and rhetoric of much Italian literature of their day. The American-influenced idioms they invented were to represent a fundamental stage in the emergence of Neo-Realism.

Neo-Realists provided some of the key moments in the representation of America as the liberator from Fascism. Films such as Vittorio de Sica's *Sciuscià* ('Shoeshine', 1946) or Rossellini's *Paisà* (loosely 'Friend', 1946), and novels such as Curzio Malaparte's *La pelle* ('Skin', 1949) mark the presence of American troops in Italy in the mid-1940s, with their cigarettes, tinned food and even black faces, as another crucial stage in America's cultural and political impact on modern Italy. But perhaps more telling still for the penetration of America as image and fantasy in the postwar era are some works from the 1950s in which a certain provincial innocence in Italy is seduced by the glamour of what America promises. The promise is not now 'epic' in scale (future riches, heroic liberation through war), but rather comic, seen in the (usually male) games and fantasies of success, charisma or escape. So, in Luciano Bianciardi's wry memoir of growing up in the dull city of Grosseto, *Il lavoro culturale* ('Cultural Work', 1957), he imagines Grosseto as a Tuscan Kansas City. And in the 1954 comedy film *Un americano a Roma* ('An American in Roma', 1954, dir. Steno), Alberto Sordi stars as a young man absurdly obsessed with all things American, from bottles of wholesome milk to Gary Cooper.

Jumping forward to the 1980s and 1990s, we find that America and Americana have taken on a quality of cosmopolitan, generic, bland modernity. Andrea de Carlo was perhaps the most lucid chronicler of this new role for America in the Italian novel. His first novel, *Treno di panna* ('Cream Train', 1981), set in contemporary Los Angeles, was written in a simple, flat style, which echoed the somewhat empty lives of the characters milling around the city and its entertainment industry. Nevertheless, the detached voice of the novel does not quite hide a residual pull of America as the very opposite of Italy, as light and unrooted. De Carlo's later novels map the concerns of his American exiles back onto the indifference of those still in Italy. And in this importing of an aura of America back into Italy, *Rimini* by Pier Vittorio Tondelli can also be included as an example, where a similar sort of Americanised cosmopolitanism casts a bland pall over the apparently glitzy beach resort.

Finally, as noted earlier, the 'cannibali' writers of the late 1990s exploited American popular culture with even more corrosive intensity, showing with bitter irony its *ersatz* importation into an Italian youth mindset. And much of the impact of the best of these (e.g. Enrico Brizzi, Niccolò Ammaniti) can be sourced, at least in their early work, to a certain clipped language and syntax aping American English (just as Pavese and others had done over fifty years earlier) and American genre writing, confirming that the 'other world' of American culture continued to fascinate and seduce Italian literature up to and beyond the century's end.

Selected reading

Pierpaolo Antonello, 'Literature and Science: Epistemological and Rhetorical Perspectives in Calvino's *Le cosmicomiche*', *Romance Languages Annual* 7 (1995), 190-8 (see section 3.2 above).

Charles Burdett, 'Visions of the United States', *MLN*, 111 (1) (1996), 164-70. About Cecchi's vision of America compared to Pavese's and Vittorini's (3.4).

Enrico Crispolti, *Il mito della macchina e altri temi del futurismo* (Trapani: Celebes, 1969) (3.2).

Emilio Gentile, 'Impending Modernity: Fascism and the Ambivalent Image of the United States', *Journal of Contemporary History*, 28 (1993), 7-29 (3.4).

Donald Heiney, *America in Modern Italian Literature* (New Brunswick: Rutgers University Press, 1964) (3.4).

David Kelley and Edward Timms (eds), *Unreal City: Urban Experience in Modern European Literature and Art* (New York: St. Martin's, 1985) (3.1).

Martin McLaughlin, 'Experimental Signs', in *Italo Calvino* (Edinburgh: Edinburgh University Press, 1998), 100-15. Discussion of *Le città invisibili* (3.1).

Luigi Monda (ed.), *L'odeporica/ Hodoeporics. On Travel Literature*, *Annali d'italianistica*, vol. xiv (1996). Themed issue of a journal on travel writing in/about Italy (3.3).

Kerstin Pilz, 'Reconceptualising Thought and Space: Labyrinths and Cities in Calvino's Fictions', *Italica* 80 (2) (Summer 2003), 229-42 (3.1).

Jon Usher, 'Primo Levi's Science Fiction and the Humanoid', *Journal of the Institute of Romance Studies*, 4 (1996), 199-216 (3.2).

John P. Welle (ed.), *Film and Literature*, *Annali d'italianistica* 6 (1988) (3.2).

4

War

For Italy – as for most of Europe, its empires and dependencies, and much of the wider world – the first half of the twentieth century was an age of war. And the violence of modern warfare was unlike that of any other age. It meant first the mass slaughter and grim trenches of the Great War of 1914-18; and then, in the Second World War, the spread of destructive technologies beyond fields of battle into programmes of systematic racial extermination and into the homes and lives of civilians, propelling the scale of death to almost inconceivable heights. The global war dead between 1939 and 1945 numbered over fifty million people.

A direct line of continuity linked these two great conflagrations of modern violence, from the fraying and then the collapse of the old, imperial world order before and during the Great War, on to the Russian Revolution and the Fascist totalitarian dictatorships of the interwar period (Mussolini, Hitler, Franco), to the Depression, the Second World War, the Holocaust and the bombing of Hiroshima and Nagasaki. This grim timeline has led the historian Eric Hobsbawm to label the first half of the twentieth century 'the Age of Catastrophe'.

The experiences of the age of catastrophe inevitably cut deep into collective and individual imaginations everywhere. They were responsible for a profoundly dark, often grotesque, nihilist or absurdist turn to the art and literature of the age (Kafka, Beckett and others). At the same time, the waves of memoir or chronicle literature that flowed from the two world wars worked to place the ordinary citizen, the private soldier, the humble victim at the heart of history perhaps for the first time. The literature of war had, to some extent, anticipated this: Stendhal's *The Charterhouse of Parma* (1839), Manzoni's *I promessi sposi*, Tolstoy's *War and Peace* (1863-9) had all shown the disorientation of war seen 'from below', by the ordinary people it sweeps up in its path. The poets of lost patriotism of the Great War and the anti-war literature of the Second World War (Joseph Heller's *Catch 22* (1955); Kurt Vonnegut's *Slaughterhouse 5* (1969)) would develop and extend this tradition. And the confusions of the ordinary individuals in war, portrayed from Stendhal to Vonnegut, would chime tellingly with the confusions and occlusions which characterise generally the fragmentation of modern identity (see Chapter 7).

To sample Italian literature's representation of and response to modern warfare, we can look in turn at three major stages: the Great War (4.1), the Second World War (4.2) and the Resistance of 1943-45 (4.3). We will also, in closing, touch briefly on representations of other forms of modern warfare and violence through the century.

4.1. The Great War (1915-1918)

Italy's response to the declarations of war of 1914 was complicated. There was uncertainty as to whether Italy would enter the war and also on which side, since she had alliances with Germany and Austria but also good reasons (which prevailed in the end) for coming in with the 'entente' powers of France and Britain. In the climate of uncertainty of this moment, a strange cluster of cultural and political forces came together to campaign for Italy to enter into the fray. Mussolini broke with the Socialist Party to campaign for intervention, thus beginning his journey towards Fascism; the iconoclastic literary figure, Gabriele d'Annunzio, made heroic speeches in favour of Italy's military destiny; the Futurists paraded their nationalist and visceral love of war, 'the world's only cleansing' (*la sola igiene del mondo*).

Italy formally entered the war in the spring of 1915 on the side of the eventual winners and so made territorial gains in the settlement at Versailles in 1919. Fighting in the north-eastern mountains around the border with Austria (the old imperial ruler of large parts of pre-unification Italy) was hard and largely unproductive, blocked in the rocks and ice, much as the fighting in Northern Europe was bogged down in muddy plains. The Italian army – fighting as a single, national, conscript force for the first time – held its ground at times, but also, famously, came close to suffering a complete rout in one of the most traumatic collective defeats in the nation's history, the battle of Caporetto of 1917. After victory, Versailles offered less territory than had been hoped for, and so became a source of regret and resentment – d'Annunzio famously called it a 'mutilated victory' – and a key factor in the birth of the Fascist movement in Milan in 1919.

Literary responses to the war, both during and after the conflict, inevitably pulled in different directions. The Futurists combined their Interventionist, war-loving politics with their modernist, experimental aesthetics to produce vivid and (in retrospect) disturbing images of war. A good illustration is a poem/collage (or 'parola in libertà', a 'word-set-free' or 'word-in-freedom') by Marinetti, still intoxicated by war as late as 1919. Its title is 'In the evening, lying on her bed, she rereads the letter from her artilleryman at the front' (see illustration overleaf). This piece is packed with telling indicators of Futurism's vision of the vitality, noise and violence of war. The explosive graphics mix shapes, onomatopoeic letters and sound patterns ('tam-tumb-tumb'), elements of synaesthesia (e.g. the mixing of colour and sound), extracts from the letter of the title ('grazie e auguri a lei e ai suoi …', 'thanks and best wishes to you and your family') and Futurist keywords or slogans ('esplosione', 'futurista', 'simultaneità', 'guerra ai tedescofili!'; 'explosion', 'Futurist', 'simultaneity', 'war to German-lovers'). Framing the whole, in the bottom right-hand corner, the silhouette of the body of the woman of the title performs a subtle task, marking the explosive quality of the rest a product of the letter (itself, therefore,

F.T. Marinetti, 'In the evening, lying in her bed, she re-reads the letter from her artilleryman at the front', 1919.

a Futurist document) and, crucially, unveiling the sado-erotic, pornographic impulse behind Futurism's celebration of war.

To the left-hand side of Marinetti's collage is a place-name we have come across before, in Giuseppe Ungaretti's poem 'I fiumi' (see Chapter 2): Isonzo. Ungaretti shared some background with Marinetti (early years in Alexandria in Egypt, a move to Paris, an experimental renewal of poetic language, later affinities with Mussolini and Fascism), but their war poetry could hardly be more different. (And both are strikingly different from the English war poetry of Rupert Brooke, Wilfred Owen, Siegfried Sassoon and others.) Ungaretti's poems are pared down, set out as short fragmented lines isolated on the white page, so that the violence of war at the frontline is one ungraspable fragment of experience alongside others. Paired with it are epiphanic flashes of something like insight or fear or illusory hope, which qualify and render even more mysterious the concrete experiences of war. Here are two such poems – 'Fratelli' ('Brothers') and 'San Martino del Carso' – written, like 'I fiumi', from the Austrian front in the summer of 1916:

FRATELLI

Mariano, il 15 luglio 1916

Di che reggimento siete
fratelli?

Parola tremante
nella notte

Foglia appena nata

Nell'aria spasimante
involontaria rivolta
dell'uomo presente alla sua
fragilità

Fratelli

(What is your regiment/ brothers?// A word trembling/ in the
night// A leaf barely born// In the agonising air/ the spontaneous
uprising/ of a man alert to his own/ fragility// Brothers)

SAN MARTINO DEL CARSO
Valoncello dell'Albero Isolato, il 27 agosto 1916

Di queste case
non è rimasto
che qualche
brandello di muro

Di tanti
che mi corrispondevano
non è rimasto
neppure tanto

Ma nel cuore
nessuna croce manca

È il mio cuore
il paese il piú straziato

(Of these houses/ nothing is left/ but some/ walls in ruin// Of so
many/ who were like me/ not even that/ is left// But in the heart/
no cross is missing// My heart is/ the most devastated land of all)

Both poems combine a stark visual scene of war (respectively, a
tense night-watch encounter and a devastated village) with some
grasp at another level, of a sense of general meaning or inner
feeling (respectively, a fragile solidarity, and inner devastation and
loss). For all that Ungaretti does not say (indeed precisely because
of the silence of the white spaces on the page), his fragments are
able to range widely and offer powerful insights into the landscape
of war and the alienating experience of its first and, in many
respects, most awful modern incarnation.

Marinetti and Ungaretti were searching for modern forms of

poetry to match the extreme nature of the war. In prose, too, the Great War produced works of unusual complexity in language and form. D'Annunzio, a figure who belongs more to the florid aestheticism or 'decadentism' of the late nineteenth century, nevertheless was still active, performing audacious stunts during the war and seizing the Yugoslav city of Fiume in 1919-20 with a private army, thus providing a key model for Mussolini. In one of his airborne exploits in the war, he lost the sight of one eye and while convalescing in the dark he wrote the strange, shadowy *Notturno* ('Nocturne', 1921). In a sequence of short, fragmentary notes, reflections and meditations, written in a prose mixing modernist allusiveness with his more usual bombastic rhetoric, d'Annunzio returns to, among other things, the death of a pilot he had flown with in the war and to a sense of the mythical power of war itself.

To balance the formal experimentalism of the works discussed thus far, we can turn now to chronicle or memoir literature. Carlo Emilio Gadda went through formative experiences of war, imprisonment and writing, chronicled in his *Giornale di guerra e di prigionia* ('War and Prison Diary', published in 1955), in a less florid style than his later work would acquire. Emilio Lussu's book *Un anno sull'altipiano* ('A Year on the High Plain') was published for the first time in 1938, as Italy was heading towards another war and Lussu was living as an anti-Fascist exile in Paris. It is a moderate and humane account of the war of his youth, and his experiences first as a footsoldier and then as a captain. The following extract recounts calmly a deeply shocking episode, in which companionship, conversation, shared memories and culture are set as starkly as possible against the meaningless, random violence of trench warfare. Lussu and his companion share a cigarette and exchange banter about why Homer's characters all drink wine and not cognac, as is the custom on the 'Altipiano d'Asiago':

'Tuttavia ... Se Ettore avessa bevuto un po' di cognac, del buon cognac, forse Achille avrebbe avuto del filo da torcere ...'

Anch'io rividi, per un attimo, Ettore, fermarsi, dopo quella fuga affrettata e non del tutto giustificata, sotto lo sguardo dei suoi concittadini, spettatori sulle mura, slacciarsi dal cinturone di cuoi ricamato in oro, dono di Andromaca, un'elegante borraccia di cognac, e bere, in faccia ad Achille.

Io ho dimenticato molte cose della guerra, ma non dimenticherò mai quel momento. Guardavo il mio amico sorridere, fra una boccata di fumo e l'altra. Dalla trincea nemica, partí un colpo isolato. Egli piegò la testa, la sigaretta fra le labbra e, da una macchia rossa, formatasi sulla fronte, sgorgò un filo di sangue. Lentamente, egli piegò se se stesso, e cadde sui miei piedi. Io lo raccolsi morto.

('And yet … If Hector had drunk a bit of cognac, good cognac, maybe he would have given Achilles more of a rough ride …'

And I too could just picture Hector, pausing for a moment after his hasty and somewhat unjustified retreat, under the eyes of his fellow Trojans sitting watching from the walls, untying from his gold-embroidered belt, a gift from Andromache, an elegant flask of cognac, and taking a drink, in full view of Achilles.

I have forgotten many things of the war, but I will never forget that moment. I was looking at my friend as he smiled, between one drag of a cigarette and the next. From the enemy trench a shot was fired. He lowered his head, the cigarette between his lips, and from a red mark formed on his forehead, a thread of blood ran out. Slowly, he slumped over and fell on my feet. I gathered him up dead.)

4.2. The Second World War (1940-1943/45)

Allied to Nazi Germany as part of the Axis, intent on expansionist, imperial adventures, furnished with its own racial politics in Africa and Italy, Fascist Italy was bound to become a central player in the Second World War. In 1939, Mussolini hesitated, aware his armed forces were far from ready, but by June 1940, after Hitler's stunning early victories, it seemed safe to join battle alongside his Axis partner.

Between 1940 and 1943, Italy fought in Southern Europe, around the Mediterranean and in Africa, contributing troops also to the terrible campaigns on the Russian front. Military failures and economic problems led to increasing discontent in Italy, however, as the Russian front faltered and Hitler's easy victory began to fade from view. Pressure reached such a pitch that on 25 July 1943, the Fascist Grand Council voted to depose Mussolini and the King had him arrested. On 8 September 1943, his successor (Marshal Bado-glio) signed an armistice with the Allies and Italy's Second World War, in formal terms at least, came to an end, to the euphoric relief of many Italians.

In reality, the fighting was far from over, and for large numbers of Italians the worst of the war was still to come. Over the ensuing eighteen months, Italy became a theatre of war, split between occupying Nazis in the North of Italy and Allied forces advancing from the South. Mussolini was reinstalled in the North as a puppet leader of a new Fascist republic (the 'Repubblica di Salò'), but the Nazis were in command; a partisan resistance campaign emerged in the same areas (see below); and the Allies fought hard battles all the way up the Italian peninsula.

As noted earlier, this war was wider ranging than the Great War in geography and also more intrusive in the lives of ordinary civilians, for both technological reasons (e.g. the scope and range of bombing raids) and political or ideological reasons (e.g. Nazi racial policies or Allied and Axis willingness to use city bombings as an instrument of war). Experiences of war and literary representations were therefore also diffuse and varied. Many of the most successful works situated their narratives at the margins of the major battles and theatres of war, from where they presented perspectives on forms of violence and destruction in war, new and old. One of the most remarkable and unexpected illustrations of this view of war from the margins came in part of Montale's third collection of poetry, *La bufera e altro* ('The Storm and More', 1956). In particular in the title poem, 'La bufera', Montale's merges his familiar imagery of a mysterious female figure with the storms, darkness and threatening destruction of war.

Another persistent concern in many responses to the war was the question of national identity, in a conflict which was fracturing the nation and its sense of patriotism and duty in very urgent ways. To give one key example of the latter, hundreds of thousands of Italian conscripts had to decide in 1943 for which Italy the Italian army should now be fighting, a fallen and corrupt Fascist Italy which had nevertheless embodied the state for so long and to which they had sworn allegiance, or a vague possibility of a future democratic Italy. *La bufera e altro* ends with an extraordinary poetic monologue, 'Il sogno del prgioniero' ('The Prisoner's Dream'), of a solider imprisoned and caught on the horns of just such a dilemma.

A sample of the literature of the Second World War, then, needs to reflect a bewilderingly wide range of experiences and sites of action. Often written in non-fictional, autobiographical or semi-autobiographical mode, literary representations took in everything from the Russian front to the German camps; from the peculiar position of Rome in the war to the experience of women; from the events of July and September 1943 to the city bombings in Italy to Italy's role in wider occupied Europe.

Nuto Revelli and Mario Rigoni Stern both lived through the Russian campaigns and wrote relatively spare and traditional narratives centred on the appalling events on that front (e.g., respectively, *Mai tardi*, 'Never Too Late', 1946 and *Il sergente della neve*, 'The Snow Sergeant', 1953). Revelli and Rigoni Stern were respected but relatively marginal figures in postwar literary circles, perhaps precisely because a pull was exerted towards Italian, civilian experiences of war, especially in the context of German occupation rather than Italian Fascist military engagement, as if the core war years themselves were somehow to be repressed from the collective memory.

For comparable reasons, the deportation of Jews and political prisoners to concentration camps was underplayed in literature, at least initially. Primo Levi's first work, *Se questo è un uomo* (1947), was famously turned down by several major publishers and read by few until it was relaunched by Einaudi in the late 1950s. And many political deportees (i.e. captured Resistance fighters) found it similarly hard to find an audience for their stories of Mauthausen and the like. There were, however, key exceptions to the rule. For example, the literary critic Giacomo Debenedetti wrote a lucid and devastating short account of the rounding up and deportation of Rome's Jews to the concentration camps in 1943. It was published in 1944, with the simple title *16 ottobre 1943* ('16 October 1943') and marks the start of a long process of integrating the persecution of the Jews in Italy into a national narrative and a national literature. Debenedetti's work can also be included with a cluster of texts – from Rossellini's film *Roma città aperta* (1945) to Elsa Morante's *La storia* (1974) – which use Rome as a key symbol of the nation and war, complicated by the role of the Vatican and by Rome's ambiguous 'open city' status at the end of the war (it was declared an 'open city' in an attempt to save it from bombardment and other war damage).

An even longer time would be needed to find a voice for the several hundred thousand Italian soldiers and civilian workers interned in German work camps after Italy's armistice with the allies. The exception to prove this rule is the 1945 play by the great Neapolitan dramatist Edoardo de Filippo, *Napoli milionaria!* ('Naples the Millionaire!'), which centres on the devastating return home from a German camp of Gennaro, who finds his family in disarray, mired in the corruptions and temptations of the black market, and his mind close to collapse. The family here stands in some way for the nation, and de Filippo locates the disorientation of war in the dual destabilisation of the ordinary (male) deportee and the family.

There is clearly a gendered aspect to *Napoli milionaria!* and it is worth underlining the increased prominence in Second World War literature of the effect of war on women's lives. This work returned more than once to an ancient, misogynist fact of war violence, rape. Rape is central to women's experience of war in work from Alberto Moravia's 1957 novel *La Ciociara* ('The Woman of Ciociaria') to Morante's *La storia* (although the experience is far more traumatic in the latter than in the former). Women are also, however, shown as agents in the war, participating in key aspects of the Resistance and the maintenance of civic consciousness as war progresses. Thus, Pina in *Roma città aperta* (famously played by Anna Magnani) and the narrator's former girlfriend Cate, in Pavese's *La casa in collina* (1948), both stand at the centre of local networks and communities which feed into the Resistance. It is at Cate's home that the community tries to fathom the meaning of Mussolini's fall and the armistice, and Pavese skilfully shows how the relief, euphoria and instinctive assumption that the war and Fascism would now end turns to a foreboding over the future. Conversely, looking at the same moment from a Fascist viewpoint, Moravia's later novel *Il conformista* ('The Conformist', 1951) reaches its climax in the chaos of Mussolini's fall: Moravia's archetypal Fascist Marcello Clerici – the latently homosexual, guilt-ridden assassin, who craves the anonymity of the crowd – sees his own fragile, conformist identity and the construct of Fascism crumble around him at the same time.

Finally, we can return to the central thread of our discussion of war literature: its depiction of forms of violence and destruction. Two texts give a sense of the two distinct protagonists of this war, the civilian and the soldier. *La casa in collina* provides us with a glimpse of the civilian experience of city bombings. Corrado, a school teacher, enters Turin after a night's bombardment:

> La mattina rientrai con molta gente in città mentre ancora echeggiavano in lontananza schianti e boati. Dappertutto si correva e si portavano fagotti. L'asfalto dei viali era sparso di buche, di strati di foglie, e di pozze d'acqua. Pareva avesse grandinato. Nella chiara luce crepitavano rossi e impudichi gli ultimi incendi.
>
> La scuola, come sempre, era intatta. […]
>
> Passò un ciclista che, pied'a terra, ci disse che Torino era tutta distrutta. 'Ci sono migliaia di morti' ci disse. 'Hanno spianato la

stazione, han bruciato i mercati. Hanno detto alla radio che torner-
anno stasera.' E scappò pedalando senza voltarsi.

(The following morning I returned to the city with many others, as
crashing and roaring noises still echoed from far away. Everywhere
people were rushing about carrying bundles. The asphalt of the
roadways was potted with holes, with coverings of leaves and with
pools of water. It was as though there had been a hailstorm. In the
clear light, the red, shameless flames of the last fires crackled on.

The school, as always, was unharmed [...]

A cyclist rode by, pausing to tell us, one foot on the ground, that
Turin was completely destroyed. 'There are thousands dead', he
said. 'They flattened the station, burned down the markets. They're
saying on the radio that they will be back again this evening.' And
he pedalled off without turning round.)

The images of everyday life – commuting into the city, the morning
damage looking like a hailstorm, school carrying on as normal,
chatting in the street – mingle with explosions in the distance, fires
burning on and warnings of thousands dead, neatly capturing the
mix of ordinary and extraordinary thrown up by this war.

La casa in collina follows a group of unexceptional individuals, on
the edge of Turin and on the edge of the war. By contrast, Curzio
Malaparte's 1945 novel *Kaputt* is set across the vast expanse of
Axis-occupied Europe and follows the military progress, the grotesque violence and the sometimes absurd socialite grandeur of the
occupying powers and their military elite. Malaparte was a war
correspondent and former Fascist (and later a Communist). His
mercurial character and his travels across Europe at war are
reflected in the dark, expressionistic style of *Kaputt*. The book is a
fascinating document of the wider European war, while also showing Malaparte slyly redeeming Italy and Italianness in the face of
both German and Russian barbarity. In the following extract, the
narrator sees for the first time the signs of defeat in the faces of the
German soldiers and in the rising mud of the Ukraine:

Pioveva da giorni e giorni, il nero e profondo mare di fango dell'Ucraina saliva lentamente all'orrizonte. Era l'alta marea dell'autunno ucraino: il fango a poco a poco gonfiava come una pasta di pane quando comincia a lievitare. [...]

I soldati tedeschi che tornavano dalle prime linee, giunti nelle piazzette dei villaggi, buttavano i fucili per terra, in silenzio. Eran coperti di nero fango dalla testa ai piedi, avevano le barbe lunghe, gli occhi infossati, e parevano gli occhi dei girasoli cosí bianchi e spenti. Gli ufficiali guardavano i soldati, i fucili buttati per terra, e tacevano. Ormai la guerra lampo, la *Blitzkrieg*, era finita, cominciava ora la *Dreissigjährigerblitzkrieg*, la 'guerra lampo dei trent'anni'. La guerra vinta era finita, ora cominciava la guerra perduta. E io vedevo nascere in fondo agli occhi spenti degli ufficiali e dei soldati la macchia bianca della paura.

(It had rained for days and days, and the black, deep sea of mud of the Ukraine was rising slowly on the horizon. This was the high tide of the Ukrainian autumn: the mud slowly swelled like bread dough when it starts to rise [...]

The German soldiers returning from the frontlines threw down their rifles, as they reached the small village squares, in silence. They were covered from head to toe in black mud, unshaven, their eyes sunken, white and deadened like the eyes of sunflowers. The officers looked at the soldiers, with their guns thrown on the ground, and said nothing. The lightning war, the *Blitzkrieg*, was over, now was the time of the *Dreissigjährigerblitzkrieg*, the 'Thirty Year lightning war'. The war of victory was over, now began the war of defeat. And I could see deep in the deadened eyes of the officers and the soldiers, the first white mark of fear.)

4.3. The Resistance (1943-1945)

The Resistance – that is the partisan campaign (or civil war) against the Fascists of the Salò Republic and the Nazis between 1943 and 1945 – merits separate attention in our discussion for at least three reasons. First, for the tens or hundreds of thousands of Italians active in it or supportive of it, it marked a dramatic break in their relations to the nation, the state and the war. Many moved from passive acquiescence to active resistance or even, as in the case of deserting army conscripts like Nuto Revelli, from active support for Fascism to active fighting against it. At both individual and collective levels, it was perhaps the single most significant source of the rebirth of a positive idea of Italian national identity (indeed, it was talked of by some as a second Risorgimento, redemption from the fall represented by Fascism). Its shared anti-Fascist ideals (despite deep ideological difference between Communist, socialist, liberal and Christian Democrat elements) largely shaped the political culture of the postwar Italian Republic.

Secondly, the experience of the Resistance and the stories told about it were crucial catalysts in the rise of Neo-Realism. Neo-Realism had many sources – in certain isolated novels of the 1930s; in radical youth Fascism; in German, French and Russian cinema; even in Fascist-sponsored institutions of culture – but it was the Resistance that transformed these disparate precursors into a moment of creativity, public 'impegno' and heartfelt shared sentiment. Many Neo-Realist texts were autobiographical accounts of Resistance experiences: and in this, they were examples of a characteristic feature of twentieth-century literature, the memoirs or chronicle by ordinary individuals who were not (or not yet) professional writers (see Chapter 6.1).

Thirdly, the literature of the Resistance was particularly important in complicating the central issue at stake in this chapter, the nature of violence in modern war. The myth and civic religion which grew up around the Resistance after the war (especially on the left), and also some literature, proposed a narrative of 'good' partisan violence – an heroic struggle for liberation against overwhelming odds, for the good of the nation (or group or class) – to be opposed to the 'bad' violence – the violence of pure power and oppression – of the Nazis and Fascists. At other times, however, writers showed an acute awareness, well before historians opened up this issue, of the moral difficulty of this narrative of the Resistance.

Two very different novels which contributed to the myth of the

Resistance, as well as fitting in with certain aspects of Neo-Realist modes of writing, were Elio Vittorini's *Uomini e no* ('Men and Not Men', 1945), centred on partisans in Milan, and Renata Viganò's *L'Agnese va a morire* ('Agnese Goes to Her Death', 1949), which tells the story of a peasant woman drawn into helping the local Resistance. *Uomini e no*, like all Vittorini's novels, is characterised by a restless formal experimentalism and complexity of ideas, whereas Viganò's follows Neo-Realist conventions more closely by being episodic, rooted in the physical landscape and in clear, everyday language. Nevertheless, both have a clear-cut sense of the rights and wrongs of the struggle they depict: the partisans are, as Vittorini would have it, 'uomini' ('human beings', or simply 'men'), whereas the enemy are monstrous, non-human in some way. It is worth noting here that this issue – the humanity or otherwise of the enemy and/or the victim – and indeed the very term 'uomo' were a crucial focal point in questions, both political and moral, about the meanings and consequences of the terrible events of the Second World War. Vittorini's title is echoed in, among other places, Primo Levi's title *Se questo è un uomo*. Furthermore, both *Uomini e no* and *L'Agnese va a morire* culminate in the deaths of their protagonists, in sacrificial acts made in the cause of the Resistance and a better future. As a result, both novels were highly successful in giving narrative shape to positive, ideological and redemptive readings of the Resistance.

The rhetoric of 'good violence', seen in novels such as these from the early postwar years, contrasts with the gently ironising emphasis on the inexpertise and youthfulness of many partisans, and on the improvised nature of many of their actions, in some other accounts. These texts began the process of constructing a more complicated and human picture of the partisan war which gathered pace in work from the 1960s. Calvino's career as a novelist began with just such as work, *Il sentiero dei nidi di ragno* ('The Path of the Spider's Webs', 1947), which centres on the experiences of a boy, Pin, his prostitute sister and a shambolic partisan group made up of former crooks. Luigi Meneghello's autobiographical work, *I piccoli maestri* ('The Little Teachers', 1964), although less comic and *faux naïf* than Calvino's, is equally effective in deflating heroic rhetoric surrounding the Resistance. Also significant here is the work of perhaps the most interesting writer of all Resistance writers, Beppe Fenoglio. Fenoglio's grandest work (compiled after his death from a complicated array of manuscripts) was *Il partigiano Johnny* ('Johnny the Partisan', 1968), an epic portrayal of the Piedmontese landscape and its partisans which, through an elaborate language much influenced by English and local dialect, manages to avoid the heroic rhetoric of other Resistance literature (although the book is not lacking in romanticising touches). Fenoglio had already published a collection of Resistance stories in 1952, *I ventitré giorni della città di Alba* ('The Twenty-Three Days of the City of Alba'), where his ironic lightness of touch was already evident. Here is the opening of the title story:

Alba la presero in duemila il 10 ottobre e la persero in duecento il 2 novembre 1944.

Ai primi d'ottobre, il presidio repubblicano, sentendosi mancare il fiato per la stretta che gli davano i partigiani dalle colline [...] fece dire dai preti ai partigiani che sgomberavano, solo che i partigiani gli garantissero l'incolumità dell'esodo. I partigiani garantirono e la mattina del 10 ottobre il presidio sgomberò.

I repubblicani passarono il fiume Tanaro con armi e bagagli, guardando indietro se i partigiani subentranti non li seguivano un po' troppo dappresso [...]. Quando poi furono sull'altra sponda e su questa di loro non rimase che polvere ricadente, allora si fermarono e si voltarono tutti, e in direzione della libera città di Alba urlarono: 'Venduti, bastardi e traditori, ritorneremo e v'impiccheremo tutti!'.

(Alba was taken by 2,000 men on 10 October and lost by 200 men on 2 November 1944.

In the first days of October, the Republican [i.e. Fascist] garrison, feeling themselves drained by the stranglehold of the partisans in the hills [...] had the priests tell the partisans that they would leave, as long as they could guarantee them safe passage out. The partisans made the guarantee and on the morning of 10 October, the garrison cleared out.

The Republicans crossed the river Tanaro with arms and packs, watching their backs to make sure the arriving partisans were not following them a little too closely [...] Then, once they had reached the opposite riverbank and nothing of theirs remained on this side except the settling dust, they stopped, turned towards the free city of Alba and shouted in unison: 'Traitors, bastards, renegades, we'll come back and hang every one of you!')

The comic vein of Calvino, Meneghello and Fenoglio was rich and subtle, but it had its limits as a means of enquiry into the Resistance and its nature as war. For the latter, Cesare Pavese comes to the fore once more, and especially his last two novels *La casa in collina* and *La luna e i falò* (1950). In the former, Corrado is gradually drawn away from Turin and into the hills in his attempt to escape the war and emotional maturity; but in the hills, he finds ever more confusion and violence. Confronted with the dead bodies of two enemy soldiers, he is forced to reflect on the levelling nature of death, as a body is no longer either a partisan or a Fascist, but a demand for an impossible explanation of war: 'ogni guerra è una guerra civile: ogni caduto somiglia a chi resta e gliene chiede ragione' (every war is a civil war: the dead are just like the living and for this, they call the living to account). And *La luna e i falò* takes this universalising sense of the violence of the Resistance a step further, culminating in the revelation of the strange, ritual death of a (woman) collaborator, who is burned by the partisans in an horrific reprise of a seasonal ritual of sacrifice. Pavese's anthropology of violence offers an alternative to the model of ideological, symbolic sacrifice 'for the cause' suggested by many Resistance narratives.

*

The Great War, the Second World War and the Resistance were undoubtedly the three greatest conflagrations of war and violence which shaped twentieth-century Italian lives; but of course, Italy experienced other battles, other phases of wars and violence, throughout the century, and these too found their way into both collective memory and literary representation. It is important to touch briefly, in concluding, on some examples of these other moments and forms of violence.

Under Fascism, for example Italy sent large numbers of troops to support Franco in the Spanish Civil War of 1936-9. For several of the young intellectuals of the day, such as Vittorini, Mussolini's intervention here was enough to turn their dissident Fascism into an embryonic anti-Fascism, as *Conversazione in Sicilia* hints at in its opening pages. Italy also undertook wars of nationalist and imperialist adventure, both before the rise of Fascism (e.g. Abyssinia, 1896; Libya, 1911-12) and during Fascism's most aggressive phase (Abyssinia again, 1935-6). The genuine public euphoria that greeted the declaration of war and empire in 1935 – the masses gathered in public squares to hear Mussolini's war speech on the radio; the women of Italy offering their wedding rings for the imperial effort – is captured in a number of literary works, including Carlo Levi's *Cristo si è fermato a Eboli* and Ignazio Silone's *Pane e vino* ('Bread and Wine', 1936). The actual experience on the ground in Africa of Italy's empire, and the cultural, social and political significance of this truncated but important phase in modern Italian history, has become a focus of interest only recently, leading to the writing and rediscovery of several literary texts set in Italian Africa (see 'Selected Reading' below).

After the Second World War, Europe entered a phase of relative prosperity and calm: Eric Hobsbawm, to contrast with his 'Age of Catastrophe', calls it 'the Golden Age'. It was, however, inevitably an age of violence also. The Cold War threw up forms of ideological violence, reflected in the intense cultural politics of a 'frontline' Cold-War state such as Italy. This was also an era built on a particular form of collective psychological violence, embodied in the real fear of the world's imminent destruction in a nuclear war. (Indeed, the Cold War sustained itself through the deterrent principle of 'M.A.D.', mutually assured destruction; nuclear war could only be avoided if both sides knew they would be annihilated by the other whenever war began.) Primo Levi's science-fiction, to give one example, is shot through with the anxieties of living under such a threat, as is the ending of his Holocaust novel, *Se non ora, quando?* ('If Not Now, When?', 1982).

A further, 'hotter' phase of violence in Italy's history left a deep mark on its collective sense of national identity in the second half of the century: the 'anni di piombo' (the leaden years), the years of extreme right- and left-wing terrorism between the late 1960s and early 1980s. The politics and cultural roots of the terrorist groupings were complex: on the left, they were in part the product of students' movements of the 1960s and of a generational rejection or radicalisation of the Resistance legacy. In a sense, this left the literary elite somewhat at a loss, and the period is commonly seen as one when mainstream intellectual culture withdrew from the 'impegno' of the postwar years. But there were important exceptions to this rule, which saw writers intensely, if problematically engaged with the crises of these years. Dario Fo's 1972 play *Morte accidentale di un anarchico* ('Accidental Death of an Anarchist'), about the death in police custody of a terrorist suspect later proven innocent, was a devastating satire of the violence of the oppressive organs of state control in the face of a terrorism created, Fo implies, by that same state. Pasolini's crusading journalism of the mid-1970s simultaneously took on the fake liberalism of the youth movements in society and the darker forces of terrorism, a stand which may well have cost him his life when he was murdered by an adolescent with unknown accomplices in November 1975. Leonardo Sciascia responded to the kidnap and assassination of Christian Democrat leader Aldo Moro with *L'affaire Moro* (1978), a subtle analysis of the workings of power, the law and the state in crisis, as well as a reading of the mind of a condemned and betrayed man, Moro, through his final, public letters. Finally, after the peak of terrorist violence had passed, works such as the title story of Antonio Tabucchi's 1985 collection *Piccoli equivoci senza importanza*

('Little Misunderstandings of No Importance') – in which judge, accused and journalist in a courtroom are all stuck playing the roles they played long ago in the hothouse of political extremism – began already the search for forms of personal and collective cultural memory of those most recent years of violence.

Selected reading

Alberto Casadei, *La guerra* (Bari: Laterza, 1999). A useful, short introduction to war in literature.

Philip Cooke (ed.), *The Italian Resistance* (Manchester: Manchester University Press, 1997). A guided anthology of documents and literary works about the Resistance (see section 4.3 above).

Donatella Della Porta, *Social Movements, Political Violence and the State* (Cambridge: Cambridge University Press, 1995). On terrorism in 1970s Italy and Germany.

David Forgacs, 'Fascism, Violence and Modernity', in Jana Howlett and Rod Mengham (eds), *The Violent Muse* (Manchester: Manchester University Press, 1994), 5-21.

William Hope, *Curzio Malaparte* (Market Harborough: Troubador, 2000) (4.2).

Mario Isnenghi, *Il mito della grande guerra* (Bari: Laterza, 1970). Influential study of intellectual and literary responses to the First World War (4.1).

Frederic J. Jones *Giuseppe Ungaretti: Poet and Critic* (Edinburgh: Edinburgh University Press, 1977) (4.1).

Helmut Peitsch, Charles Burdett and Clare Gorrara (eds), *European Memories of The Second World War* (Oxford: Berghahn, 1999). Contains several interesting essays on Italian representations of the Second World War (4.2).

The Public Sphere

Pirandello's groundbreaking philosophical novel *Il fu Mattia Pascal* (1904), as we have seen before, ends with the hero's failure to construct a new identity for himself as 'Adriano Meis' and his subdued return to his home town. But for all the novel's philosophising, what defeats Mattia in the end is not so much a weakness of will or of self (although there is that also), as the insurmountable obstacles thrown up by petty bureaucracy. Unable to denounce a crime against him, unable to contemplate marriage, unable even to own a dog, all because he does not exist in the official files of police and state, Mattia/'Adriano' limps home (where he is bureaucratically certified as already dead). Conversely, in a 1911 short story 'La patente' ('The License'), Pirandello shows how public bureaucracy (here, a court) can stamp with official existence even the most absurd and nonsensical practice; in this case, the 'evil eye' of one of his characters.

This aspect of Pirandello's work caused discomfort amongst critics who expected grand, lyrical ideas from their literature, not bureaucracy. But, in retrospect, these works look prescient: they point us to a crucial aspect of the experience of modernity, to the area where private lives meet and are shaped by the public sphere, by the organs, institutions, spaces and structures of the state. This terrain would become a central feature of both modernist literature (epitomised by Kafka) and modern political reality, especially in the extreme coercion and control of individual lives by the state under totalitarian régimes such as Fascism.

The workings of the public sphere define and determine individuals' lives in a wide range of different ways, in complex interaction with inner processes of definition and perception. To gain some perspective on this, we can look at literary representation of three distinct types of public institution: institutions of politics or power at the 'highest' level (the state, government, political parties, the Church) (5.1); institutions of social control, ordering and surveillance, whose function is to discipline and to punish (the police, the army, courts, prisons, hospitals, asylums) (5.2); and the institutions of socialisation, education and belief, which shape norms and values rather than specific acts of behaviour or regulation (the family, the home, school, the workplace, the Church again) (5.3).

5.1. The state

The key area to explore under this heading is, inevitably, Fascism. Under Fascism, both policy and political philosophy pointed to the supremacy of the state over the individual. Mussolini's power and mythical status was such that he embodied the state; the organisations of government, education, the economy and local surveillance all emanated from an ideal of the state; a chain led relentlessly upwards from the individual to the mass to the Party, *Duce* and state. In a sense, then, under Fascism, the distinctions between levels of the public sphere set out above dissolved into the all-encompassing ideal of the state (although the ideal was not successfully realised in practice, by any means). Such was the very definition of the totalitarian state (a term coined by the philosopher of Fascism, Giovanni Gentile).

All this suggests that the role of the state under Fascism was both elusive and ubiquitous, both an 'idea' or an 'ideal' pervading people's lives and the more familiar practical authority of the law. Two anti-Fascist novels (more telling, in this respect, than pro-Fascist novels) attempt to portray the pervasiveness and also the often tawdry reality of the Fascist state as it impinged on people's lives: Ignazio Silone's great anti-Fascist parable, *Fontamara* (1933), and Alberto Moravia's analysis of the mind and motivation of a Fascist, *Il conformista* (1951).

Fontamara tells the story of a village in the Abruzzi region whose inhabitants fall victim to the machinations of local politicians and landowners. Reacting with perplexity and stubbornness, and without an ounce of political consciousness, to measures which, for example, cut off the water supply to their land, they find themselves branded as subversives. The turns of Silone's story are at times comic (there are scenes of near slapstick comedy and absurdity, such as when the villagers are called upon to declare their allegiance to the proper authorities, of whom they are quite unaware) and at others terrifying in their violence (there are scenes of rape, torture and murder by local thugs and criminals absorbed into state militias). Layers of the Fascist state (petty officials, violent squads, local authorities such as the 'podestà', and so on) emerge as they impose themselves on this isolated, poor community. The effect is akin to dramatic irony, as the readers see through the naivety of the villagers to an understanding of the mechanisms of Fascist power: a compound mixture of the oldest, crudest forms of local wealth, privilege and criminality, bound together with new forms and degrees of regimentation, spectacular politics (seen in the grand parade in a nearby town) and ruthless state violence. For all its simplistic narrative modes and black-and-white morality, *Fontamara* contains in allegorical form a sensitive analysis of the insidious spread of the Fascist state down to the lowest and most isolated levels of society. Silone would translate this analysis into more articulated form in later works of the 1930s, including the mock-political-dialogue *La scuola dei dittatori* ('The School for Dictators', 1938).

Fontamara offers a vision of the strange contours of the Fascist state from the perspective of the marginalised and excluded. This perspective is repeated in other spheres, such as in several important novels which have explored the Fascist exclusion of Jews following the 1938 Racial Laws (for example, Giorgio Bassani's *Il giardino dei Finzi-Contini*, 'The Garden of the Finzi-Contini', 1962;

parts of Primo Levi's *Il sistema periodico*, 1975; Rosetta Loy's *La parola ebreo*, 'The Word Jew', 1997). Few works of literature, however, have attempted to penetrate the structures and ideology of the Fascist state from within, from the centre rather than from the margins. Moravia's *Il conformista* is a significant exception. Although its primary interest is a psychological, or rather psycho-sexual, analysis of an individual Fascist, Marcello Clerici, who vacillates between being a figure for the Fascist everyman and a 'perverse' exception to all norms, *Il conformista* shows Marcello moving through the institutions and often hidden centres of power of the Fascist state. A key early scene takes him to an imposing Fascist ministry building, where he spies on the minister in his grandiose office having sex, and mixes with a ragbag of functionaries and appellants of the state – from seedy agents to old professors to garish prostitutes – who repel him, just as his minder later in the novel, Orlando, a typical, boorish Fascist enforcer, will repel him. The ministry building itself – with its waiting rooms, disused halls, interconnecting doors and corridors which allow Marcello to spy unobserved as he waits – evokes the labyrinth of the Fascist state, its duplicity and hidden structures and its moral vacuity. In a later scene, the state seems to be allegorically pictured in the mental asylum where Marcello's father is held believing he is a minister of the Fascist state, with his slogan 'Strage e malinconia' (Slaughter and Melancholy).

In postwar Italy, the state was, of course, nothing like the authoritarian power it had been under Fascism. Nevertheless, a government dominated by one party (the DC) and a polarised and strongly clientelist party politics made for a persistent sense that an insidious web of state power – the hidden state – continued to control society. This view became particularly prominent in the 'anni di piombo' when many came to believe that forces close to the centre of the state (secret services, mixed with Masonic, mafia and/or neo-Fascist groupings) had been working to destabilise democracy in Italy. The hidden state, and the secret machinations of the police in enforcing it, was satirised in many of Dario Fo's broad-brush comedies. More subtle were the attempts to get inside the covens of the secret state and the party system, to understand the careful balancing act between legitimate and illicit power, in Leonardo Sciascia's 1970s novels, *Il contesto* ('The Context', 1971) and *Todo modo* (1974; the title is Spanish, meaning roughly 'Any Which Way'). The latter is set at an isolated spiritual retreat, run by the charismatic and devious priest don Gaetano, which acts as a cover for the meeting and machinations (and extra-marital affairs) of DC power-players: ministers, cardinals, industrialists, newspaper editors. Sciascia inserts an outsider, an artist, as his narrator, there to witness as the guests begin to be murdered. The webs of secrecy are never uncovered, but don Gaetano provocatively hints at the essential significance of these meetings and of the effects of this form of politics, the dissolution of the state in a hall of mirrors of hidden power:

'Lo stato non è un borsaiuolo', disse con indignazione il ministro.

'Certo, non è un borsaiuolo', confermò, con piú moderata indignazione, il presidente.

'Ma signori', disse don Gaetano al ministro e al presidente, 'spero non mi darete il dolore di dirmi che lo stato c'è ancora … Alla mia età, e con tutta la fiducia che ho avuto in voi, sarebbe una rivelazione insopportabile. Stavo cosí tranquillo che non ci fosse piú.'

Il ministro e il presidente istantaneamente, d'un rapido sguardo che si scambiarono, decisero di prenderla come una facezia. Risero. Ridevano ancora quando ci alzammo da tavola.

('The state is not a petty thief', said the minister indignantly.

'For sure, it is no petty thief', the president confirmed, with a milder form of indignation.

'But sirs', said don Gaetano to the minister and the president, 'I hope you will not be so cruel as to tell me that the state still exists … At my age, and after all the faith I have had in you, it would be an unbearable revelation. The idea that it was no longer there was so calming.'

The minister and the president, in the instant it took for them to exchange a look, decided to treat it as a joke. They burst out laughing. And they were still laughing when we got up and left the table.)

5.2. Prison, army, hospital

According to a schema conceived by the influential French historian Michel Foucault, the key contours of modern society since the Enlightenment can be drawn by observing those public institutions which regulate and keep under surveillance potential dangers to society and deviations from its norms. Such 'dangerous' figures include the weak, the sick and the insane; the criminal; and the sexually wayward or 'deviant' (especially among women and the young). And the institutions which evolved in their modern forms to regulate and control them range from schools, prisons and armies to hospitals and asylums. Certain of these are constructed and function as discrete, closed-off worlds, where coercion and control are much stronger than in wider society (e.g. prisons, asylums). These are blind spaces, inaccessible to the 'normal' individual, but with a presence and meaning clear to all. Other such institutions work as microcosmic reflections of the wider society, intersecting at various points the lives of many or most individual citizens of the state (e.g. schools, hospitals, conscript armies). These intermediary, highly symbolic institutions straddle the border between the private and the public spheres of modernity; and this borderland is one that literature has patrolled and mapped out in many different ways.

Limiting ourselves to three examples – prisons, armies and hospitals – we can first look for literary texts which illuminate specific aspects of modern Italian history and society, from the perspective of one of these institutions; and then for texts which interrogate in a less contingent, more abstract manner their structures and meanings as regulatory, disciplinary spaces.

Prison literature has an established pedigree in Italy, at least as far back as Silvio Pellico's account of his ten years in an Austrian prison during the early Risorgimento, *Le mie prigioni* ('My Prisons', 1832). In Chapter 4, *Il giornale di guerra e di prigionia* (1955) by Carlo Emilio Gadda was mentioned, where the author relates his experiences in prison after being captured by the Austrians in the Great War. But, as one might expect, it is the period of Fascism, the war and its aftermath which produces the twentieth century's most characteristic prison literature, or what followers of Foucault would call 'carceral' literature. One form of imprisonment very particular to the Fascist régime, which inspired an impressive array of memoirs in the years following, was the practice of sending subversives into 'confino', or internal exile, in deeply isolated rural areas. The strange encounter of anti-Fascist intellectuals and activists with the cultures and practices of the rural South, coupled with their odd status as guests, with a certain degree of freedom of movement and thought, but always under surveillance and control, made for fascinating narratives in works such as *Cristo si è fermato a Eboli* by Carlo Levi (1945) or Cesare Pavese's *Il carcere* ('Prison', 1948).

By far the most significant and influential prison-writer of the Fascist period, however, was not a literary figure at all. Antonio Gramsci spent eleven years between 1926 and 1937 in various prisons, closed houses, internment camps and prison hospitals, only to die shortly after his final release. Over this time, he worked away at a series of prison notebooks reflecting on his Communist ideology and on Italian history, literature and culture. When published after the war, these *Quaderni del carcere* ('Prison Notebooks') helped to redefine first Italian Communism and then a great swathe of Communist and leftist thought (especially about the role of culture and the intellectual) in Europe and beyond. But even before the *Quaderni* began to appear in 1948, Gramsci became known and widely admired, even idolised, as the author of *Lettere dal carcere* ('Letters from Prison', 1947), subtitled in some editions 'Un carattere per gli italiani' [A Character for Italians], a series of letters which painted a moving picture of his prison life and his relations with family and friends outside. Besides the emotional richness of the letters, they are interesting as prison literature (despite not being literary in any narrow sense) for their charting of the different prison regimes Gramsci moved through, for the different networks and contacts between prisoners, and for the individual resilience of the mind of a long-term and increasingly sick inmate. Here is an extract from a letter to his wife Giulia in 1930, which mixes light and dark in articulating his sense of isolation, of a slowing of time and the weakness of the prisoner's contact with the outside world:

Nella nostra corrispondeza manca appunto una 'corrispondenza' effettiva e concreta: non siamo mai riusciti a intavolare un 'dialogo'. le nostre lettere sono una serie di 'monologhi' che non sempre riescono ad accordarsi neanche nelle linee generali. [...] Ricordo una novellina popolare scandinava: - tre giganti abitano nella Scandinavia lontani uno dall'altro come le grandi montagne. Dopo migliaia di anni di silenzio, il primo gigante grida agli altri due: 'Sento muggire un armento di vacche!'. Dopo trecento anni il secondo gigante interviene: 'Ho sentito anch'io il mugghio!' e dopo altri 300 anni il terzo gigante intima: 'Se continuate a far chiasso cosí, me ne vado!''. Beh! non ho propria voglia di scrivere, c'è un vento di scirocco che dà l'impressione di essere ubbriachi.

(In our correspondence, there is precisely no concrete, real 'correspondence': we have never managed to sustain any real 'dialogue: our letters are a series of 'monologues' which are rarely in tune with each other even in general terms [...] I am reminded of a popular Scandinavian story: three giants are living somewhere in Scandinavia as far apart from each other as the great mountain peaks. After thousands of years of silence, the first giant shouts to the other two: 'I can hear a herd of cows mooing!'. Three hundred years later, the second giant speaks up: 'I heard the mooing too!'. Another 300 years and the third giant says sternly: 'If you carry on making all that noise, I'm leaving!' Well, I can't bring myself to write today, there's a scirocco wind blowing which makes you quite lightheaded.)

Also published in 1947 was Primo Levi's first account of his eleven months in Auschwitz, *Se questo è un uomo*, an account which lays out with devastating clarity the extremes of humiliation of the prisoner and the extremes of pedantic, near absurd orderliness of the prison system of the concentration camp. We will look more closely in Chapter 7.4 at Levi's analysis of the disintegration of the self as part and parcel of this horrific modern experiment in mass murder. Here, it is worth noting his remarkable sensitivity to the institutional microcosm of the prison world – pushed to appalling extremes in Auschwitz: its opaque, closed off, but fiercely applied rules emanating both from above and from the society of prisoners; the fundamental importance of hierarchy, again both imposed (political prisoners first, Jewish prisoners last) and internally created (longstanding prisoners before new arrivals); the key role played by language, including a sort of prison jargon born of the babelic mix of the camp; the spontaneous creation of internal markets, in which food, scraps of comfort, particular jobs or privileges are bartered and bought in whatever currency is of value (bread, soup, protection); the almost complete dissolution of bonds of solidarity; the transformation of morality (stealing is a norm) and even physiology (feet injuries can kill, diseases such as dysentery are commonplace); the delusory collective silences or fake consolations that all prisoners share. These elements, and many more, build up in *Se questo è un uomo* into a sociology and social psychology of a world which is somehow both wholly alien and inverted with respect to the outside, 'normal' world which produced it, but also deeply, disturbingly aligned with that normal world.

As seen in Chapter 4, the experience of the modern soldier – conscripted, regimented and thrown into wars where codes of individual combat are rendered all but irrelevant by technology and/or ideology – has something in common with the experience of the prisoner. The absurdity of the situation and the conditions of such lives – touched on by Levi also – is evoked with allegorical power in a novel which appeared in 1940 (just before Italy entered the Second World War) and which is commonly seen as the most 'Kafkaesque' work in modern Italian literature, Dino Buzzati's *Il deserto dei Tartari* ('The Desert of the Tartars'). Buzzati's hero, Giovanni Drogo, is called up for a short period of military service in a desert fort where the Tartars threaten to attack. They never do, but Drogo never manages to leave the fort, dragged into its routines and hierarchies, unable to defeat the logic of its system. Meanwhile the fort fades into a ruin around him:

> Dalla pianura del nord non si ammetteva eventualità di minaccia, tutt'al piú poteva comparire al valico qualche carovana di nomadi. Cosa sarebbe diventata la vita lassù?
>
> Meditando a queste cose, Drogo raggiunse nel pomeriggio il ciglio dell'ultimo pianoro e si trovò la Fortezza davanti. Essa non chiudeva piú, come la prima volta, inquietanti segreti. Non era in verità che una caserma confinaria, un ridicola bicocca, le mura non avrebbero resistito che poche ore ai cannoni di recente modello. Con l'andar del tempo sarebbe stata lasciata andare in rovina, già qualche merlatura era caduta e un terrapieno si sfasciava in frana senza che nessuno lo facesse aggiustare.

> (From the northern plain no threat could be expected, at most some nomad caravans might appear at the pass. What would become of life up there?
>
> Pondering these things, Drogo reached the edge of the plateau by afternoon and saw the Fortress before him. Unlike the first time, it no longer held disturbing secrets. It was in fact no more than a border barracks, a ridiculous hovel, whose walls would not have survived more than a few hours of attack from the more recent models of cannons. As time passed, it would be left to fall into ruin, already bits of battlements had fallen off and an embankment had broken up in a landslip without anyone rebuilding it.)

All the military discipline had been an illusion, to control and give order to the lives within; thus *Il deserto dei Tartari* can work as an allegory for the coercions of all modern life, for the routines of work (see below) and the absence of glory and meaning.

As if to confirm the analogies between the various institutions under scrutiny here, Buzzati also explored the hospital in a short story, 'Sette piani' ('Seven Floors', 1942) (later rewritten as a play, *Un caso clinico*, 'A Medical Case', 1953), in which a bewildered patient finds he is relentlessly transferred from floor to floor, signifying a movement to ever graver levels of sickness, culminating in terminal illness. And indeed, there are several instances of works which intermingle more than one of the institutions of army, prison, hospital, asylum and others: the asylum scene in *Il conformista* would be one; another worth mentioning is Aldo Palazzeschi's strange Futurist satirical novel, *Il codice di Perelà* ('Perelà's Code', 1911), in which the hero, a man literally made of smoke, moves through the royal court, the law courts, the prison, the army and more, as he is commissioned to rewrite the legal 'Code' (hence the title), causing mayhem as he goes; and in Calvino's short novel, *La giornata di uno scrutatore* ('A Day in the Life of an Election Scrutineer', 1963), Turin's asylum the 'Cottolengo' is transformed for a day into an electoral seat, and the institutions of the hospital, the political parties (especially the PCI) and the democratic state mingle confusingly, leaving the intellectual protagonist more than a little disconcerted.

5.3. Home, family, work

The institutions of the state, of parties and the like are in a sense intangible, but are certainly located outwards and upwards from individuals' lives. Hospitals, barracks, prisons are, literally, sites elsewhere, often on the edge of towns and cities as they are on the edge of lives. But within ordinary lives also, the patterns of family life, everyday work and other quotidian activities can themselves take on functions of social regulation. Everyday institutions – 'the home', 'the family', 'work' – the sites of normality, which the institutions of exclusion and control of the previous section are designed to protect. It is telling that, in *Il conformista*, these are the aspects of life Marcello struggles so hard to get right in order to seem normal (his bourgeois marriage and home, his keen willingness at work), and which he gets so wrong by trying too hard to be normal. In this sphere, the balance between private and public tilts towards the private, where much literature naturally settles also, but it is a privacy and an intimacy subject to larger, outside forces.

The home and the family are the first and most longlasting 'social' influences on the formation of the self. They loom large in modern literature; indeed, they could be said to be constitutive of the modern form of literature *par excellence*, the novel. From early in the century, writers used the family as an arena within which to explore indirectly the larger insecurities of identity and social positioning thrown up by modernity. A key early example was Pirandello, who persistently used private family roles and the public conventions attached to them to set challenges to his characters' sense of self and social position. Questions of fidelity or infidelity, maternity or paternity, conjugal happiness or unhappiness, dignity or indignity, filial loyalty or disloyalty, love or hate – and, most often, the conflict between the reality and appearance of any or all of these – recur again and again as instruments of comic and/or tragic drama in his work. (Examples of plays touching on these themes would include *Il piacere dell'onestà*, 'The Pleasure of Honesty', 1918; *Tutto per bene*, 'All For the Best', 1920; *La signora Morli, una e due*, 'Signora Morlì, One and Two', 1920; *La vita che ti diedi*, 'The Life I Gave You', 1923.) And in this focus on the family, Pirandello sets himself on a cusp, showing a society partly constrained by old systems of honour and public face (rooted in his Sicilian background) and a modern instability of family relations and of the private sphere in which relations falter before his characters' and audiences' eyes.

Pirandello investigates the family (as he does other institutions and social practices) as a structure in the system of identity formation and deformation, and on this basis, his work builds into an exploration of the modern world. He is not, in other words, a realist, directly intent on painting a faithful picture of the modern family. Turning to Alberto Moravia's striking first novel, *Gli indifferenti* ('The Indifferent Ones', more commonly translated as 'The Time of Indifference', 1929), we find something closer to a realist's portrait of a middle-class family, although one not without philosophical tinges (the book has been compared to the existentialist narratives of Sartre and Albert Camus), and indeed, in the eyes of many, political tinges (if the family stands for the Italian bourgeoisie under Fascism). Looking through the eyes of Michele Ardengo, the disaffected protagonist of the book, the reader witnesses the tortuous, claustrophobic and ultimately vacuous configurations of relationships within the family, from his jealous mother Mariagrazia and her cynical lover, Leo, to the resentful children, failed rebel Michele and Carla, whom Leo eventually seduces and marries. The circuitry of the family relationships is deadening and all action precluded: indifference applies first of all to Michele, but ultimately to the entire value-system embodied in this empty but cluttered milieu.

Michele's moody contemplations of his own family serve to place him in narrative terms in a privileged position, both insider and outsider, just as many Pirandellian protagonists use their wit and insight into the workings of identity to rise above the constraints of the institution of the family. Both authors tended (with notable exceptions) to privilege male protagonists of this kind. Over the course of the twentieth century, however, it has been particularly women writers, and the analysis of gender roles in the family and the home, which have produced the most telling insights into this social institution. Put schematically, if the family as a social formation had been explored by male and female writers alike, then the home, as the space and institution on which the family is based, was opened up and dissected most forcefully by women writers. And the political implications of this work showed the public power and influence of these apparently private institutions, the construction and constrictions of gender roles and identities as played out first there and later on the larger stages of public life.

This applies to the line of explicitly feminist literature across the century, from Sibilla Aleramo's *Una donna* (1906) – with its portrait of the oppressive, patriarchal, provincial family, first of the protagonist as child and then as wife and mother – to Franca Rame's dramatic monologues, *Tutto casa, letto e chiesa* ('Nothing But Home, Bedroom and Church', 1977), which stage the neglect and exploitation of the mother/wife in her relations with her husband, her work, her children, her body and her sexuality. And it applies no less strongly to declaredly non-feminist women writers, such as Natalia Ginzburg, who perhaps did more than any other writer of the century to shape new narrative voices – voices of colloquial clarity and studied social banality beneath which intense emotional lives are played out – through which to listen to the semi-private world of the family. Ginzburg carried this out in her fiction (e.g. *Tutti i nostri ieri*, 'All our Yesterdays', 1952; *Le voci della sera*, 'Voices in the Evening', 1961), in her later chronicle of the author of *I promessi sposi* and his family, *La famiglia Manzoni* ('The Manzoni Family', 1985), and most famously, in her autobiographical work, *Lessico famigliare* ('Family Sayings', 1963). The latter was built around her memories of her family, which happened to have been engaged in important anti-Fascist activities as she was growing up, thus making her autobiography a public, historical document as well as a private act of memory. *Lessico* claims privacy for these events by filtering them through the private language of the family 'lexicon' of the title – the words and phrases, nicknames and stock terms which peppered family conversation – pinpointing the key role played by language at the border of private and public spheres, in binding together home and family, in the present and as memory.

Our final example of an everyday place and practice, which is shared by the most ordinary of lives, and constitutive of self and society in the modern world, is the workplace. Of all the institutions under scrutiny in this chapter, this is perhaps the easiest of all to label along a spectrum that goes from the traditional to the modern, and this makes it an especially useful tool for a literature engaged with modernity. Thus, there is a strong, if minor body of literature which holds on to the rhythms and values of ancient patterns of work: this includes a literature of rural life and the peasantry, written at the moment of its decline (e.g. by Ferdinando

Camon), but also work such as Primo Levi's *La chiave a stella* ('The Wrench', 1978), which celebrates a modern version of the wandering, artisanal craftsman – here embodied in the industrial rigger Libertino Faussone – proud of his pragmatic, problem-solving skills and stubborn wisdom. This form of work is a direct challenge to the nihilistic slogan Levi saw at Auschwitz's gate, 'Arbeit macht frei' (Work sets you free):

> Il termine 'libertà' ha notoriamente molti sensi, ma forse il tipo di libertà piú accessibile, piú goduto soggettivamente, e piú utile al consorzio umano, coincide con l'essere competenti nel proprio lavoro, e quindi nel provare piacere a svolgerlo.

> (The term 'freedom' notoriously has many meanings, but perhaps the type of freedom that is most accessible, most personally enjoyed, and most useful to human society is the type that comes from being good at one's own work and so taking pleasure in carrying it out.)

Levi maintains something of the same view of his own work as a laboratory scientist, first as a student and later at work in a paint factory, described in his autobiography *Il sistema periodico* (1975), where the challenges of solving the riddles of the compounds and their practical consequences for materials is represented as profoundly satisfying, even natural, a sort of modern incarnation of hunting and survival.

If the artisan and the peasant were figures in decline, new workplaces and new forms of work emerged, as did new forms of literature to understand them, most often in much less idealising terms. Perhaps the two emblematic modern workplaces for the mass of individuals in the twentieth century were the office and the factory. The work of the office emerges early in the literature of the century, and especially from the 1950s onwards, as the epitome of standardised, dull, modern life. Svevo's first and third novels, *Una vita* ('A Life') and *La coscienza di Zeno*, are steeped in the atmosphere and degraded tensions of office work, in a bank and a family business respectively. In *Il sistema periodico*, Levi soon shows his disaffection with his work, when he moves up the company ladder and so away from the lab and into management offices. In Calvino's short novel, *La nuvola di smog* ('The Cloud of Smog', 1959), the protagonist's encounter with the city, with modern life, and with the insidious pulviscular pollutions that come with it, begins in the cluttered, dusty office of the magazine he works for, and, more particularly, at his desk:

> I primi giorni di lavoro all'Ente li impiegai a mettere in ordine la mia scrivania. Il tavolo che m'era stato assegnato era infatti carico di roba: fogli, corrispondenza, cartelle, vecchi giornali; insomma, era stato fin allora una specie di tavolo di sgombero su cui venivano posate le cose che non avevano un posto preciso. Il mio primo impulso era stato quello di far piazza pulita; ma poi avevo visto che c'era del materiale necessario per il giornale, e altre cose che dovevano avere un certo interesse e che mi ripromisi d'esaminare con piú calma. Insomma finii per non togliere niente dal tavolo e invece aggiunsi molta roba però non in disordine, anzi cercavo di tenere tutto ordinato. Si capisce che le carte che c'erano prima erano molto polverose e comunicavano la loro polverosità anche alle carte nuove. [...] nel giro di pochi giorni prendevano un aspetto vecchio e sporco e dava noia a toccarle.

> (I spent my first days at work for the Institute organising my desk. I had been assigned a table piled up high with stuff: papers, correspondence, folders, old newspapers. In short, up until that point, it had been used as a sort of clearing point, for anything which had no precise place elsewhere. My first impulse was to sweep it all away, but then I saw that some of the material was needed for the newspaper, and other things were interesting in their way and I promised myself I would look them over when I had a quiet moment. So, in the end, I left the table as it was, and instead added a great deal more stuff, although not in a mess; on the contrary, I tried to keep it all very ordered. Of course, the papers that were there before were all very dusty and they passed on their dustiness to the new papers [...] in the space of a few days, they all took on an old and grubby look so that it was unpleasant even to touch them.)

Calvino combines a close attention to detail and distinction here with a comic emphasis on the loss of order and control, on the dust and decay at the heart of these apparently new, efficient workplaces.

The factory has a particular place in modern Italian literature, since the question of how literature should deal with industry, its sites and spaces became a hotly debated issue around the early 1960s in intellectual circles of the left. The key document here was a special issue in 1961 of the journal edited by Vittorini and Calvino, *Il menabò*, on literature and industry. Several writers close to these circles tried their hand at integrating industry into their work, from Ottiero Ottieri's *Donnarumma all'assalto* ('Donnarumma on the attack', 1959) to Nanni Balestrini's *Vogliamo tutto* ('We Want it All', 1971): the most successful was Paolo Volponi, beginning with *Memoriale* ('Report') which appeared in 1962. *Memoriale* follows from within the devastating decline of the Piedmontese factory-worker Albino Saluggia, as his paranoia and instability of mind (rooted in his time as a prisoner of war) are exacerbated by the impenetrable world of the factory and the abyss which separates it from his rural home. As with the offices of Svevo and Calvino, Volponi's factory contains seeds of a sickness or pollution which can be broadly identified as a symbol of modernity itself, although none of these writers is interested in apocalyptic denunciation. They rather create images of the complexity and difficulty, the challenges to the very core of identity, thrown up by apparently banal and repetitive practices of modern work.

By the end of the century, neither the factory nor the office loomed particularly large in the literary imagination: in the case of the former because it was on its way to becoming a somewhat outdated image of the workplace; and in the case of the latter because it had, in contrast, become almost banal and unremarkable. What is replacing them is a more fluid mobile vision of work, blurring the boundary between home and the workplace, through technology such as the personal computer, the internet and the mobile phone. However, the effects of the 'virtual' realities created by such technologies on the public sphere and its interface with private identity, are, for now, still being explored most fully in genres such as science-fiction rather than in mainstream narrative.

Selected reading

Guido Bonsaver and Robert Gordon (eds), *Culture, Censorship and the State in 20th-Century Italy* (Oxford: Legenda, 2005) (see section 5.1 above).

Ann Caesar, 'Configurations of Identity: the Family's Undoing', in *Characters and Authors in Luigi Pirandello* (Oxford: Oxford University Press, 1998), 101-32 (5.3).

Mirna Cicioni, *Primo Levi. Bridges of Knowledge* (Oxford: Berg, 1995), 70-96. On Levi's work-related books, *Il sistema periodico* and *La chiave a stella* (5.3).

Michael Hanne, 'Silone's *Fontamara*: Polyvalence and Power', *MLN* 107 (1) (January 1992), 132-59 (5.1).

Massimo Lollini, 'Literature and Testimony in Gramsci's Letters from Prison: The Question of Subjectivity', *Canadian Review of Comparative Literature* 23 (2) (June 1996), 519-29 (5.2).

Ellen Nerenberg, *Prison Terms* (Toronto: Toronto University Press, 2001). Looks at representations of prison and confinement in Italian literature during and after Fascism (5.2).

Judy Rawson, 'Dino Buzzati', in Micheal Caesar and Peter Hainsworth (eds), *Writers and Society in Contemporary Italy* (New York: St Martin's Press, 1984), 191-210 (5.2).

Sharon Wood, 'Memory and Melancholy in Natalia Ginzburg', in *Italian Women's Writing 1860-1994* (London: Athlone Press, 1995), 135-51 (5.3).

6

Other Voices

6.1. Identity literature

Chapter 1 offered a rough sketch of the figure of the writer in twentieth-century Italy, asking 'where' and 'how' she/he typically carried on her/his activities as both artist and cultural operator. This suggested the foundations for a sort of sociology of the modern literary field. But in order to characterise the modernity of twentieth-century literature in itself, as literature – what set it apart from the traditional forms and voices of past literatures, how it revolutionised itself over the course of the century – another question needs to be put: not only 'where?' and 'how?', but also 'who?'.

In more than one sense, the writer's social identity often came to be *the* defining feature of both writer and work in the twentieth century. (This is to leave aside for now the philosophical and formal questions of identity or selfhood which, as we will see in Chapter 7, were central to so much modern literature.) First, literature increasingly opened itself up to voices or categories of individuals who had traditionally been excluded from the literary élite or the cultural establishment, indeed from society's centre more generally. Previously, the question 'who is writing?', asked of a contemporary work of Italian literature, would more often than not elicit the response: white, Italian, heterosexual, highly educated, of a certain age, middle- or upper-class and male. By the end of the century, the answer would often have to be strikingly different, including epithets such as: female, poor, young, averagely educated, gay, foreign or ethnically diverse.

This broadening of the constituency of literature was a direct product of the mass literacy, mass education and broad prosperity of modern Italy; and of the mass migration of people and cultures that blurred borders and ethnic identities. Both writers and readers took in a vastly wider spectrum of society by the end of the century as a result. So much was this so that at times the gender, sexuality, age or provenance of authors could be quite irrelevant to their writing, even if it was sociologically significant; and many preferred it that way. This is not to say, however, that the experiences of being female, poor, young, averagely educated, gay, foreign or ethnically diverse were no longer fraught with difficulty. On the contrary, in many instances, the shaped expression of writers' experiences of exclusion, subordination and oppression became the essential substance and value of the literature they produced (even against the intentions of the authors). This identity literature, at its most self-conscious and political, was a form of testimony, a literature which let other voices be heard and, over a period, changed the contours of literature itself as a result.

We will look below at some of the voices to emerge during the twentieth century through identity or testimonial literature, broadly conceived. But before addressing these, we can usefully return to their intellectual forerunner and point of origin in the nineteenth century: the literature of the poor. Ever since Manzoni chose to centre *I promessi sposi* on Renzo and Lucia, two humble, poor, uneducated villagers and their travails in the face of the evil aristocrat don Rodrigo; ever since Verga eschewed his sophisticated 'Northern' narrative style in favour of stories about the desperately poor and suffering peasants and fishermen of his native Sicily; ever since d'Annunzio tapped into the grotesque, violent beauties of the Abruzzi as a resource for his symbolist poetry, drama and narrative, Italian literature has shown something of a vocation for immersing itself in the intensely non-literary world of the poor. The problem with this vocation – aesthetic and moral-political – was the status of the poor with respect to the voices of the text depicting them. For as long as the voice came from outside and above the world being represented, it laid itself open to accusations of populism, of treating the poor as object rather than fully-centred subject of the text, whether the populism came in the form of a certain paternalistic condescension (Manzoni), a mythical vision of the poor as out of time, out of history (Verga) or a folkloric aestheticisation of local customs (d'Annunzio).

The problem was, of course, in part with literature itself: as soon as the poor are given literary voice, they lose authenticity. It was also symptomatic of the 'top-down', pedagogical nature of national identity and culture in the unified Italy, made *for* the people rather than *by* them. How, then, to give voice to the people, and how to mediate between culture and the people? By far the most influential formulation of the problem in the twentieth century came from the cultural politics of the left, thanks to the extraordinary work of Antonio Gramsci.

The role of culture within Marxist ideology, in Italy but in due course also far beyond Italy, was transformed by Gramsci's *Quaderni del carcere*. In particular two Gramscian notions became common currency in the language of cultural debate, both of them part of a response to that tricky question of how to mediate between culture and the people. The first − 'national-popular' culture − described a culture that might manage both to embody national identity, in some unified but neither homogenising nor hierarchical way, and to address and give voice to the people as a whole, including or especially the poor, the uneducated, exploited working and peasant classes. The second − the idea of the 'organic' intellectual − envisaged the intellectual not as the educator of the people into culture, but rather as something like the opposite: that is, the articulator of the already-rich culture, philosophy and ideology of the people, the means through which the people acquired an analytical consciousness of its own culture. The intellectual would be of the people, 'organic' to it rather than structurally superior to it.

Soon after the publication of the *Quaderni*, there was an evident Gramscian tinge to several literary projects of the postwar period. For example, working separately in the mid-1950s, both Calvino and Pasolini produced anthologies of popular cultural forms around the Italian peninsula – Calvino worked on folktales (*Fiabe italiane*, 'Italian Folktales', 1956), Pasolini on dialect poetry and popular song (*Poesia dialettale del Novecento*, 'Twentieth-Century Dialect Poetry', 1952; *Canzoniere italiano*, 'Italian Songbook', 1955). Both were stitching together something very much like 'national popular' texts, drawn out, analysed and articulated organically from within popular culture. And both took the lesson of their anthologies and used them in their own work: Calvino's trilogy of fables, *I nostri antenati* ('Our Ancestors', 1952-9), that was to launch the second non-realist phase of his career; and Pasolini's novels, stories and films set in the slum suburbs of Rome, using carefully recorded dialect.

These were still, self-evidently, highly literary projects, written in a 'low' voice, but not quite of or by the people (although Pasolini encouraged several of his 'ragazzi di vita' into writing or cinema careers). Over the course of the century, it became possible for the people themselves to write their own lives and stories. As Chapter 4 suggested, modern wars in particular (and especially in the Italian case, the Resistance of 1943-45) opened up this path and testimonial literature, by non-professional writers, emerged first of all here.

Gramsci's model remained an ideal rather than an achieved form of literary practice, however. A genuine literature by the poor was rare: one famous example which did succeed was *Padre padrone* ('Father Boss', 1975; later filmed by the Taviani brothers), a vivid autobiographical account by Gavino Ledda of his grim, desperately poor, illiterate, rural Sardinian childhood and his escape from it. But *Padre padrone* was more the exception than the rule. The poor, especially the rural poor, ceased to be the central focus of this kind of literature in the postwar period, as the centre of the culture as a whole shifted dramatically towards the urban and the modern. Instead, other categories of subaltern, silent, excluded or oppressed groups, came much more strongly to the fore. In an international context, this included the late twentieth-century trend of postcolonial literature, through which the voices of ex-colonial subjects and cultures became central to English, French and other literatures. In both Italy and elsewhere, these were not simple phenomena, and the otherness of the new literary voices often hid privileges as bourgeois and conventional as the 'dead white males' they challenged, but they undoubtedly marked a sea change in the function of identity within literature as within society. We will examine their presence and impact in Italy under four headings: gender (6.2), youth (6.3), homosexuality (6.4) and other cultures (6.5).

6.2. Gender

One of the most striking developments in twentieth-century Italian literature has been the emergence of women writers to take the very centre stage of the literary scene, and to do so in such substantial numbers that (paradoxically) the literary market at the end of the century was all but gender-blind.

Although there had been a rich vein of women writing in humanist and/or Petrarchist mode during the sixteenth century, the tradition of women's writing in Italian up to and including the late nineteenth century was a relatively weak one. Where women did write, their work was often precluded from normal channels of publication, dissemination and, therefore, canonisation. From the late nineteenth century up to and throughout the Fascist period, however, there were clear signs of change, as women writers were able to enter an expanded market for books and women readers were important in an increasingly literate population. Women writers found success both in popular literary genres, such as romantic and children's fiction, and in the sphere of socially committed and realist writing (e.g. Matilde Serao and Grazia Deledda), although under Fascism, feminist thinking was not welcomed (Alba De Cespedes fell foul of censors with her first novel, *Nessuno torna indietro*, 'No one Goes Back', 1935, for this reason). There was a handful of Futurist women and even a Futurist manifesto for women (despite the open misogyny of the main players in the movement). But perhaps the pivotal text of this period was Sibilla Aleramo's *Una donna* (1906).

Una donna, a work already mentioned more than once, is a useful and prescient text for understanding Italian women's writing of the twentieth century for a number of reasons. First, it uses the *Bildungsroman* genre (that is, the story of the formation and entry into maturity of the young protagonist) and self-consciously moulds it to make its endpoint a new, emancipated female intellectual identity. This journey to emancipation has aspects of the heroic to it, but Aleramo is careful to underscore the compromises, risks and losses (most poignantly, and some would say melodramatically, of her son) along the way. The genre of the journey to emancipation through loss and guilt would recur in politicised works of the 1970s in and around the feminist movements and key debates over divorce and abortion legislation at that time, such as Oriana Fallaci's *Lettera a un bambino mai nato* ('Letter to an Unborn Baby', 1975). Echoing the climax of *Una donna*, Fallaci's novel is a tale of the sacrifice of a son for the mother's autonomy, although here the son is still in the womb, and the issue is abortion rather than abandonment. So powerful is the guilt engendered by possible motherhood and possible termination that Fallaci has her protagonist imagine herself literally on trial.

Una donna also touches on several crucial symbolic aspects of the subordination of women under patriarchy – the silencing of women; sexuality, rape and the law; the mother-daughter relationship, women's insanity (here of the protagonist's mother) – which would all feature prominently in later feminist literature and politics. (Indeed, *Una donna* itself would be recovered as a text of literary interest in the 1970s.) To give a handful of examples from the 1970s and after: the issue of insanity and hysteria and its imposition as a social position on women was central to the feminist movement, and found a writerly expression in works such as Giuliana Morandini's ... *e allora mi hanno rinchiusa* ('... And So They Locked Me Up', 1977), a collection of testimonies from women inmates of mental asylums; silence, rape, the law and writing feature prominently in

Maraini's *La lunga vita di Marianna Ucrìa* (1990); and the mother-daughter relationship was a leitmotif of a number of richly complex novels of this period, such as Sanvitale's *Madre e figlia* (1980) or Fabrizia Ramondino's *Althénopis* ('Althenopis', 1981).

It would be a mistake, however, to equate the rise of women's writing in the twentieth century with a rise in feminist conscious-ness. Many women writers (including some of the most politically committed, such as Maraini) felt uncomfortable with the label feminist and several rejected it outright. Similarly, it would be a mistake to jump too neatly from the first wave of agitation for women's voices to be heard at the turn of the century to the second wave in the 1970s. In between, a rich field of literary achievement by women writers is to be found, fed by contact with European writing in the interwar years (several women writers translated and read Virginia Woolf, Katherine Mansfield and others), and emerg-ing in its own right and with great energy in the postwar years. The same years that saw the peaking and fading of the (largely male-dominated) Neo-Realist movement, also saw the appearance of Natalia Ginzburg's family narratives (see Chapter 5); works of both chronicle and visionary imagination by Ortese; Elsa Morante's complex narratives of isolation and fantasy (*Menzogna e sortilegio*, 'Lies and Sorcery', 1948; *L'isola di Arturo*,1957); and Anna Banti's intimate and baroque dialogue-cum-imagined-autobiography *Artemisia* ('Artemisia', 1947).

An important open question remains as to whether the distinct concerns, styles and modes of narrative on display in this array of work – centred variously on the private, the fantastic, the hidden, on desire and the body, and only obliquely connected to history, society and public world – could ever amount to a 'feminine' or female voice for literature ('écriture féminine', as it was labelled by French theorists), determined by gender as much as any explicitly feminist work. It could be argued that the very styles of writers such as Ginzburg or Banti (both of whom rejected the label of 'feminist') introduce elements distinct from the traditional aesthetic criteria of what constitutes literary language. The following two extracts are strikingly different in style, but each in their way might be said to pull literary language into new, possibly feminising directions:

> – Sai, mi ero un po' innamorata di quel violinista.
> – Che violinista? – lui disse.
> – Giorgio Tebaldi.
> – Ah.
> Lui disse, dopo un lungo silenzio:
> – Ci hai fatto l'amore?
> – No, – lei disse, – no.
> Ma il cuore le pesava come un sasso, per aver mentito.
> A volte si metteva a piangere, quand'era sola; e diceva:
> – Ma perché sono cosí disgraziata?
>
> Ginzburg, *Le voci della sera*

> ('You know, I'd fallen a little bit in love with that violinist.'
> 'Which violinist?', he said.
> 'Giorgio Tebaldi.'
> 'Oh.'
> After a long pause, he said:
> 'Did you make love with him?'
> 'No,' she said, 'no'.
> But her heart weighed her down like a rock, because she had lied.
> Sometimes, when she was alone, she cried, and said:
> 'Why am I so miserable?')

Non potrò piú liberarmi di Artemisia, questa creditrice è una coscienza puntigliosa e ostinata a cui mi avezzo come a dormire in terra. Non è piú il colloquio dei primi giorni a impegnarmi, ma una specie di patto stipulato in regola fra notaio e testante: a cui devo fare onore. Frattanto posso distrarmi, esercitare certe malizie su un ricordo che, ormai, dissimulo. Disse Orazio, 'Ti devi sposare'. Ma io già trascino Artemisia a spasso per i giardini di Boboli strapazzati e deserti dopo l'esodo dei profughi; e la costringo a muoversi insieme agli ultimi rimasti, tristi padroni di un grande spazio contaminato, a incontrarci prostitute e soldatacci; a bagnarcisi di pioggia autunnale. Il ritmo della sua storia aveva una morale e un

senso che forse son crollati con le mie ultime esperienze. Io me li
gioco: si contenti, Artemisia, di quel che viene.

Banti, *Artemisia*

(I will never free myself from Artemisia. She is like a creditor, a
stubborn, headstrong conscience whom I have become used to as I
am used to sleeping on the ground. Ours is no longer the dialogue
of the first few days, but more like a pact drawn up with due process
between a notary and a testator: a pact I must respect. In the
meantime I can amuse myself, playing certain tricks with a memory
that, now, I cover up. Orazio said, 'You must marry'. But I am
already dragging Artemisia off on a stroll through the Boboli gar-
dens, left battered and empty after the refugees' departure. I force
her to move around amongst the last remaining figures, grim
masters of a great, contaminated space, to meet with prostitutes and
bedraggled soldiers; to get wet in the autumn rain. The rhythm of
her story had a moral and a meaning, but they have perhaps
collapsed along with my most recent experiences. I will take the risk:
and Artemisia will have to take what comes.)

Ginzburg's style is marked by oral, intimate and inconsequential
elements; Banti's by fluid, associational elements, focused on an
imaginary female friendship. Both contrast with the norms of
sequential drama, conflict, public action and strong character
which conventional (and therefore male) narrative might demand.
But then, gender aside, modern or modernist literature was also
challenging such norms and conventions at this time. Whether or
not such contrasting voices could be said to come together as
feminine in some way, then, they certainly suggest that women
writers were often at the forefront of modern innovations in literary
language.

6.3. Youth

The case of the literature of youth is somewhat different from the
others under consideration in this chapter, since youth is not quite

a category of social exclusion in the same way as gender, sexual orientation and cultural difference have been. Nevertheless, the opening up of the literary field to previously unheard voices and cultures of youth has been one of the most remarkable cultural changes of the century.

The modern fascination for youth has taken many distinct forms. In the late nineteenth century, there were strong manifestations of a certain Romantic myth of innocence and purity surrounding the figure of the child. For example, the poet Giovanni Pascoli, a key figure in the transition to a modern poetic diction, published an essay in 1903 called *Il fanciullino* ('The Small Boy'), in which the poet's intuition and vision was likened to that of the child. Pascoli's child influenced the less sentimental boyish qualities of Umberto Saba's autobiographical poetry and the (eroticised) young boys of the poetry of Pasolini and Sandro Penna (see below). And generally, the realm of the child remained a privileged site of memory, nostalgia and escape in narrative for many writers (see Chapter 2.2.1). It was, however, the figure of the youth or the adolescent (often conceived as anything from teenage to the age of forty) and the growing importance of the collective category of the (young) generation as a player on the cultural stage, which was to have the greater socio-cultural impact. So, for example, the vitality and iconoclasm of several of the new intellectual groupings and movements at the start of the century was bound up with their youth: the Florentine group around the journal *La Voce* and its predecessor *Leonardo*, including Prezzolini, Papini and Soffici, were all in their twenties and explicitly conceived of their project of cultural renewal as a generational one. Marinetti's founding manifesto of Futurism proclaimed the centrality of youth to the Futurist project: 'The oldest among us are thirty [...] When we are forty, we hope other, younger and stronger men will throw us in the bin, like so many useless manuscripts.' Here, the ideology of modernity as permanent revolution and renewal which frequently lies behind the rhetoric of youth is made explicit; and both the rhetoric and the ideology were shared by totalitarian movements such as Fascism.

The Fascists invested heavily in a cult of youth, with all the strength, athleticism and idealisation of the (most often male) body that this implied. The regime marshalled the nation's youth into militarised, regularised shape, training both the body and the mind in preparation for battles ahead (real or imagined) and the glorification of the nation. Part and parcel of this cult was the youthful vigour of the 'Duce' himself, depicted in newsreels and the like, skiing, riding horses and working in the fields. And alongside the cult of the body, the regime also harnessed the intellectual energy of youth, for example in its university movements (the GUF and the GIL) whose meetings and competitions ran both physical and cultural events in parallel. It was in these ambits that many of the future writers and intellectuals of the postwar era, such as Vittorini and Pratolini, were formed. Vittorini's first novel, *Il garofano rosso* ('The Red Carnation', 1933) was steeped in the youthful, violent energy of the Fascist squads and their revolution. The younger Fascist intellectuals of the 1930s tended to gravitate towards a less conservative politics (often labelled 'fascismo di sinistra') than that of the regime; and from this position, many moved over to outright anti-Fascism and to leftist ideologies at various points before or during the war. As a result, on-going debates in Fascist intellectual journals about the role of the young in Fascism, such as in the journal *Primato* (1940-43) run by Giuseppe Bottai, were in reality seedbeds for post- or anti-Fascist culture.

In the second half of the century, the role of youth in culture reflected deep changes in a modernising Italian society in which the young (first men and subsequently, in a slower process, women too) were becoming more educated, more prosperous and more independent from their families. A publishing phenomenon which illustrated the challenges to the status quo presented by the young was don Lorenzo Milani's *Lettera ad una professoressa* ('Letter to a School-Mistress', 1967), a critique by schoolchildren of the Italian school system. In this context, it was no longer either small groups of young intellectuals or top-down official institutions and rhetoric which gave shape and expression to the category of the young; but rather a youth culture shared by swathes of an entire generation, with broader and looser cultural reference points than those of the Italian literary élite. An emblematic illustration of the mutual incomprehension between older intellectuals and the new youth culture was the famous polemical poem by Pasolini, 'Il PCI ai giovani!!' ('The PCI to the Young!!'), written in response to the 1968 student movement, in which Pasolini acknowledged that his generation had been superseded by the students, violently criticising them as middle-class pseudo-revolutionaries, and siding against them and with the police who had beaten them: they at least, Pasolini declared, were genuinely poor sons of Southern peasants.

1968 and its long aftermath – from the student and workers' movements of 1968-69 and 1977 to the terrorism, political extremism and social campaigns of the 1970s – represented, in a sense, the unleashing of the new generational power of youth. Within this ferment, literature and other forms of cultural expression retained a significant role. Forms of 'samizdat' culture grew up within the movements (songs, leaflets, street theatre, posters and cartoons, alternative radio, super 8 video) and influenced the writers who emerged from the movements (just as Neo-Realism had been influenced by the clandestine Resistance news-sheets of the 1940s). *Porci con le ali* ('Pigs with Wings', 1976), by Lidia Ravera and Marco Lombardo Radice (under the pseudonyms Rocco and Antonia), was a sensational sexual satire on '68. New youth genres emerged, such as so-called 'cyberpunk' writing. A generation of novelists reflected the wave of youth activism of the late 1970s, including Enrico Palandri, whose *Boccalone* ('Loudmouth', 1979) centred on Bologna in 1977; and Gianni Celati, teaching at Bologna at this time, emerged as a key figure of influence for this youth-centred narrative, for works such as *Lunario del paradiso* ('Paradise Almanac', 1978).

Another figure formed in the Bologna of 1977 was Pier Vittorio Tondelli, whose important early work *Altri libertini* ('Other Libertines', 1980) gave vivid expression to the drug-filled youth sub-culture and who went on to write about the hedonistic vitality of youth of this phase, relatively immune to ideology (e.g. *Un weekend postmoderno*, 'A Postmodern Weekend', 1990). But more importantly here, before his premature AIDS-related death in 1991, he worked at a series of anthologies of young writers, nurturing and editing his authors, and publishing them under the title *Under 25* (from 1986). The *Under 25* volumes uncovered a vein of very young writers, and reopened the possibility of literature as a potentially relevant form of expression for the young. This led, more or less directly, to 1990s phenomena such as the 'cannibali' and to youth-oriented, multi-media book series such as 'Stile libero', the cleverly packaged and marketed Einaudi series which launched the 'cannibali', as well as cleverly repackaging potential youth 'gurus' such as Fo and Pasolini. In among the marketing games, however, genuinely important cult phenomena emerged, such as Enrico Brizzi's vibrant debut *Jack Frusciante è uscito dal gruppo* ('Jack Frusciante has left the group', 1994).

6.4. Homosexuality

The representation of homosexuality in Italy, especially male homosexuality, has a long tradition associated with the Platonic, pedagogical conventions of male friendship in ancient Greece; and an almost equally longstanding tradition of repression and victimisation by the Church, state and society. As a result, homosexuality and homoeroticism were an ambiguous presence beneath the surface and at the margins of Italian literature from its inception, from Dante and Boccaccio onwards. Into the twentieth century, it remained commonplace to code homosexuality as deviant, corrupt, abnormal and/or duplicitous, and this in arenas well beyond the sexual: thus, both Rossellini's film of 1945, *Roma città aperta* and Moravia's *Il conformista* (1951) equate homosexuality with Fascism and betrayal. During the course of the century, however, mostly under cover at first and increasingly openly towards the end, the homosexual voice (again, mostly male) began to be heard prominently within Italian literature. The tale is not quite one of emancipation ending in open acceptance, though, since within literature and within society old prejudices were hard to displace.

We can look at instances of three phases of the positioning of the homosexual voice and the representation of homosexual desire *from within* over the course of the century. The earliest phase, and the hardest to document, takes in the first half of the century when the taboo on the subject was still strongly in force and representations were oblique or private; and yet, in memory at least, this period at times emerges as one of almost idyllic innocence. Both Umberto Saba and Pasolini wrote short novels (thinly veiled as fiction in both cases) about their youthful homosexual experiences, set in the late 1890s and 1940s respectively; and both left these novels incomplete and unpublished during their lifetimes. They were published post-humously, Saba's *Ernesto* ('Ernesto') in 1975 and Pasolini's *Amado mio* (the Spanish title, meaning 'My Love', taken from a popular song sung by Rita Hayworth in the 1946 film *Gilda*) in 1982. Although writing from very different perspectives and in varying tones of intensity, the two writers both throw an aura of youthful innocence and initiation over the love stories they tell, leaving an undertow of anxiety and guilt very much as a subtext. Saba uses his characteristic ironic touch and direct narrative style, rooted in dialogue, related from the point of view of his adolescent, innocent hero 'Ernesto', as he is initiated into sex and a nascent self-con-sciousness; Pasolini's work deploys a more charged, bucolic and sensual style, as he relates a sun-drenched summer's tale of intense desire in the Friulan countryside. Both succeed in 'normalising' – rendering simple, inevitable, natural – their narratives of homo-sexual desire and love, but only in these hidden texts.

A poet close to both Saba and Pasolini at different times – Sandro Penna – was able to write more openly about his sexuality (surprisingly so, given he began writing in the 1930s), in a style of clarity, rhythmic simplicity and intensity. He perhaps represents the sign of a transition to a more direct and vocal phase, as shown in this simple poem from his 1939 collection, *Poesie* ('Poems'):

Trovato ho il mio angioletto
fra una losca platea.
Fumava una sigaretta
e gli occhi lustri avea …

(I found my little angel/ down in the seedy stalls./ He was smoking
a cigarette/ and his eyes were glistening …)

Shortly before his death, Pasolini provocatively recalled the idyllic
aura of the hidden world of momentary happiness and innocence
of the pre-war era, in a review of Penna's poetry: he described Italy
under Fascism as a 'wonderful country', because for all the regime's
persecution and control, desire could at times be played out in all
innocence, whereas by the 1970s, a public tolerance of alternative
sexual mores was in fact a veil for a hypocritical, consumerist
conformism which destroyed the possibility of innocent, heterosexual or homosexual desire.

Pasolini's work as a whole and his very public and controversial
career as an intellectual, poet and filmmaker, means he was a key
figure also in a second phase of expression of homosexuality in
modern Italian literature, a phase of still deeply ambivalent and
problematic grappling with the issues and experiences of homosexuality, but one now projected, at least partly, into public arenas
of expression. Until the final years of his life, Pasolini only rarely
declared his homosexuality or identified himself in any positive or
constructive way as gay. However, homosexual desire was everywhere in his work, close to the surface, sublimated and sublime: see,
for example, his very physical poetry about the body of Christ and
about being an outcast, a 'diverso' (as in the poem 'La Crocifissione', quoted in Chapter 2); or the sexual servicing of older men
by the young boys who people his Roman novels such as *Ragazzi di
vita* (1955); or the bisexuality of the Christ-like guest figure in the
novel and film of *Teorema* ('Theorem', 1968); and so on. The
rhetoric of 'scandal' produced by all this, which pervaded Pasolini's
work and life, was first and foremost a code for the challenge
represented by his homosexuality to social and cultural conven-

tions. But the code was not theorised or politicised or, very often, even made explicit. Only in the very final period of his life did Pasolini seem to change gear, picking up on the liberalisation of social attitudes of the 60s and 70s (even though he despised it) and writing more openly about his sexuality; the peak of this was to have been reached in the array of extremely explicit sexual scenes and practices spread through his vast unfinished ideological novel, *Petrolio* (only published as a posthumous fragment in 1992). In this he also placed himself (or began to do so before his murder cut short the process) at the birth of a third phase in this history, a phase of a literature centrally and openly concerned with contemporary gay sexuality and identity.

The two key figures for this final phase were Pier Vittorio Tondelli and Aldo Busi. Both born in the decade following the war, both began publishing successful novels with explicit homosexual themes (rooted in autobiography and the narrative of the subcultures they frequented) in the early 1980s. Tondelli's early works, *Altri libertini* and *Pao Pao* (after the acronym for the army-unit where the book's hero is doing his military service, 'Picchetto armato ordinario', 1982), both contain vivid homosexual elements. Before his death, Tondelli attempted a more conventional and restrained narrative in *Camere separate* ('Separate Rooms', 1989), centred on a gay couple, one of whom is dying of AIDS. Although the novel falls rather flat as narrative, it is undoubtedly a milestone in its emotional maturity, its subtle representation of a pattern of mourning and its insight into the tensions and prejudices still dogging the life of a gay couple. Busi is quite another matter, temperamentally and stylistically: he has produced a prolific amount of work since his striking and elaborate first two novels, *Seminario sulla gioventù* ('Seminar on Youth', 1984) and *Vita standard di un venditore provvisorio di collant* ('Standard Life of a Temporary Tights Salesman', 1985), all of it exhibiting a high level of linguistic play and experimentation, coupled with bacchanalian, provocatively explicit displays of gay sex.

Finally, the loosening of taboos on sexuality has also led to the beginnings of a lesbian literature in Italy, in certain areas of genre literature and in cult books such as Elena Stancanelli's 1998 novel *Benzina* ('Petrol').

6.5. Other cultures

Italy was largely monocultural – white and Catholic – in its race, religion and ethnicity until the final decades of the twentieth century. Multiculturalism was another aspect of twentieth-century modernity to arrive late and with difficulty here (although, as explained in Chapter 1.1, Italy has always had its own forms of internal cultural and linguistic diversity). There was a handful of very small ethnic communities distinct from the dominant culture, such as the Slavs on Italy's long-contested north-eastern frontier or the Waldensian (non-Catholic Christian) community which survives still in the north-west, or the Albanians in Sicily. In twentieth-century literature, some writers from these communities have used their ethnic identity and its tensions with their Italianness to underpin their work, as with the Italo-Slav writer Fulvio Tomizza. The oldest minority community of all has been the 40,000 or so Jews, present in the peninsula since Roman times. From within the Jewish community, a strikingly rich line of modern writers emerged (including Saba, Svevo, Moravia, Bassani, Ginzburg, Primo Levi, Carlo Levi, Franco Fortini), although for many of these, their Jewish or partial Jewish ancestry was a relatively minor aspect of their identity and work.

Italy as a nation has, of course, contributed to modern, global multiculturalism on a massive scale, through emigration. Italian ethnic clusters grew up throughout the world and contributed, for example, to an extraordinarily successful global and commercial culture of Italian fashion and food, Italian-American cinema and literature, and so on. The phenomenon of emigrant return means that elements of other cultures were imported into Italy at ground level (see Chapter 3.4 for the example of the spread of American culture). And it is also true that, in the twentieth century as in the eighteenth or sixteenth, an international artistic élite has used Italy as a base for its cultural explorations and imported its own influences along the way into the local cultural sphere.

Immigration to Italy from other countries remained on a very small scale until the late 1980s. There is a handful of isolated, but significant examples of immigrants who brought alternative cultural coordinates into Italy and into Italian literature before the eighties. Take the case of two Jewish-Hungarian writers, both born in the 1930s: Edith Bruck and Giorgio Pressburger. Bruck survived deportation to Nazi concentration camps, drifted around various countries after the war, including Israel, before settling in Italy in 1954 where she published her first autobiographical work (begun in Hungarian but completed in Italian), *Chi ti ama così* ('Who Loves You Like This', 1958). Bruck's Italian is dark and direct, her stories typically violent in emotion and experience: her use of an alienating other language allows her to become an alienating voice of another history and culture within Italian literature. Pressburger left Hungary, with his twin brother Nicola, at a later crisis point, after the Russian invasion of 1956. His first work, co-written with his brother, *Storie dell'ottavo distretto* ('Stories of the Eighth District', 1986), evokes the Budapest they left behind in quirky, witty tales.

Immigrant writers such as Bruck and Pressburger are very much exceptions for the larger part of the twentieth century. But in the late 1980s, legal and illegal immigration (predominantly from North and West Africa and Eastern Europe) grew into a significant phenomenon in Italy for the first time. The life-threatening boat journeys, the individual, institutional and political racism encountered once within Italy (giving the lie to an older myth of Italians' 'immunity' to racism), the difficulties of creating multicultural openness in a previously monocultural society: all these problems became prominent in the news media and also prompted some of the immigrants to write accounts of their experiences in the language of their new country. Thus, a minor wave of immigrant literature began around 1990, which, although mostly promoted by very small publishers and selling in small numbers, stood out as one of the defining features of Italian literature of the 1990s, because of its unprecedented injection of a dimension of ethnic and cultural pluralism into the Italian novel. At first, these accounts were co-authored or 'ghosted' by Italian journalists or writers: this was the case with the two key works of 1990, Salah Methnani's *Immigrato* ('Immigrant'), co-written with Mario Fortunato, and Pap Khouma's *Io venditore di elefanti* ('Me, An Elephant-Seller'), co-written with Oreste Pivetta. Soon, immigrant authors writing on their own also appeared: for example, Mohsen Melliti's *I bambini delle rose* ('The Children of the Roses', 1995) or Shirin Ramzanali Fazel's *Lontano da Mogadiscio* ('Far from Mogadishu', 1994). Of course, the styles and approaches of each text were distinct, even as they tackled the common struggles of the immigrant and used these to gain a perspective on the host society and culture.

As one critic, Jennifer Burns, has argued, this body of work is held together by its very fragility: by its fragile relationship with the Italian language, by the fragile guest-host negotiations with Italian culture in these authors' lives and writings, by the fragile status of immigrant identity, torn between memories of home and impulses to integration, and by the physical fragility of the immigrant's body, at risk of violence at any turn. Burns also suggests that this wave is fragile in that its monothematic nature might lead to its fading after a short time. Even if that were the case, these authors nevertheless represent a distinctly identifiable continuation of the much longer history of the literature of testimony and identity in the twentieth century, through which literature has become a means to make heard the subordinate, forgotten or marginalised voices within Italian culture.

Selected reading

Alberto Asor Rosa, *Scrittori e popolo* (Turin: Einaudi, 1988; 1st edition 1965). Influential polemical account of modern Italian literature's approach to 'the people' (see section 6.1 above).

BASILI at http://www.disp.let.uniroma1.it/basili2001. Online database of immigrant writing in Italy (6.5).

Marco Belpoliti, 'Carnevale a Bologna', in *Settanta* (Turin: Einaudi, 2001), 235-71. On the cultural and literary milieu of the Bologna movement of 1977 (6.3).

Jennifer Burns, *Fragments of 'impegno'* (Leeds: Maney, 2001). Interesting discussion of Italian narrative 1980-2000, touching on youth writing (6.3), Tondelli (6.4) and immigrant writing (6.5).

Andrea Ciccarelli, 'Frontier, Exile and Migration in the Contemporary Italian Novel', in Peter Bondanella and Andrea Ciccarelli (eds), *The Cambridge Companion to the Italian Novel* (Cambridge: Cambridge University Press, 2003), 197-213 (6.5).

Derek Duncan, 'Pier Vittorio Tondelli: An Art of the Body in Resistance?', *Italica* 76 (1) (Spring 1999), 54-69 (6.4).

Francesco Gnerre, *L'eroe negato: omosessaulità e letteratura nel Novecento italiano* (Milan: Baldini & Castoldi, 2000). Survey of gay writing and representation in modern Italian literature (6.4).

Antonio Gramsci, *Selections from Cultural Writings*, edited by David Forgacs and Geoffrey Nowell-Smith, translated by Willian Boelhower (London: Lawrence and Wishart, 1984) (6.1).

Letizia Panizza and Sharon Wood (eds), *A History of Women's Writing in Italy* (Cambridge: Cambridge University Press, 2000). Modern era covered in Part III, 149-281 (6.2).

7

The Fragmented Self

In Chapter 6 and at several other points in this book, questions of identity in literature have emerged as central to the century's literature, where identity has variously indicated the sociological origin of authors, their position within the literary field, their sexuality or gender, their specific experiences (of war, trauma, prejudice, subordination to institutions and power, and so on). This 'identity politics' has been one of the central channels through which literature has encountered and interrogated modernity in the twentieth century. To complete the picture, however, we need to open out a further, wider perspective on the whole question of identity: that is, we need to explore the distinctly modern processes and ideas by which the very notion of the unitary, human individual, or the self, was variously questioned, weakened, relativised, obscured, split, dismantled or destroyed. This chapter looks at some of the key motifs and manifestations of the fragmented self in modern literature.

The late nineteenth century in Europe was marked by a number of philosophical and psychological currents – derived from figures such as Darwin, Kierkegaard, Nietzsche and Schopenhauer – which tended to challenge certainties and decentre received wisdom about the self, humanity, God and the world around us. Each filtered through to the modern consciousness of the self, and literary expressions of it, in crucial ways; but, as the very word 'consciousness' might suggest, probably the key figure in this context (and certainly a key illustrative example) was Sigmund Freud, and his invention and vigorous promotion of psychoanalysis from the 1890s onwards.

Well before Freud, from at least as far back as Descartes, a self split between mind and body had been a commonplace of philosophy; but Freud radically undermined even this binary model, suggesting that in the unconscious mind and in the complex interactions between it and the conscious mind, a vast and almost indecipherable zone of uncertainty existed. He suggested that the self was in some way always absent to itself, split and in dramatic conflict with itself, uncertain and unsettled. This, his conception of psychopathology and the so-called 'talking cure', his emphasis on involuntary actions and slips of the tongue, on dreams and jokes, on childhood and sexuality set at the heart of the new understanding of the self processes richly exploitable by literature: conflict, language, memory and narrative, desire, multiple levels and codes of meaning, metaphor. It is thus not surprising that, even as Freud's reputation as a psychologist sank towards the end of the twentieth century, after a period of massive influence, his impact on literature remained extremely potent.

As in many other areas of external intellectual influence, Italy's reception of Freud was slow at first and then rapid and distorted later on, as frenetic efforts were made to tap into international trends. The translation and dissemination of his work in Italy was severely limited in the first half of the century. Only after the Second World War would his work begin to be translated and read closely; and only with the new intellectual currents of the 1950s and 1960s would it enter the mainstream of Italian intellectual life. Throughout, large parts of the spectrum of Italian culture – from Croce to the Fascists, from the Communists under Togliatti to intellectuals near to the DC – remained deeply suspicious.

There were, however, notable exceptions: in Trieste, the city's geographical and cultural proximity to Vienna brought early contact with psychoanalysis for writers such as Svevo and Saba; a small number of exceptional critics such as Giacomo Debenedetti were already using Freud in the 1920s and 1930s; Gadda's *La cognizione del dolore* ('The Knowledge of Pain'), which appeared in instalments between 1938 and 1941, is clearly influenced by Freud's ideas on taboo and patricide; and Pavese's theories of myth were as much influenced by Jung as by anthropologists such as J.G. Frazer and Mircea Eliade. And, more generally, the shape and nature of what are now thought of loosely as Freudian conceptions about the self and identity permeated Italian literature of the century. We can pick out four archetypes of the fragmented self as it emerges in modern literature, influenced by Freud and other modern philosophers of the self: the antiheroic figure of the weak or failed self (7.1); the self as divided, hidden or unhinged (7.2); the self in memory (7.3); and the shattered self (7.4). In examining these archetypes, the focus will be on exemplary works, all from the first half of the century, by four key writers – Svevo, Pirandello, Montale and Primo Levi – which were influential in mapping out the territory for modern explorations of the self.

7.1. 'Un inetto'

Here are six snippets of quotations or situations from key works of Italian literature published before 1925. Italo Svevo's first novel, *Una vita* (1892), tells the story of the ineffectual moves in Trieste's upper-middle-class circles of bank clerk Alfonso Nitti, leading to his suicide. It was to have been entitled at one stage 'Un inetto', 'An Inept Man'. Pirandello's *Il fu Mattia Pascal* (1904) ends with its protagonist so detached from the world as to seem half-dead, the 'late' Mattia Pascal. Guido Gozzano's poetry, in *I colloqui* ('Conversations', 1911) and other collections, pictures a series of *alter egos* who are variously grown old before their time ('Venticinque anni … Sono vecchio, sono/ vecchio!'; 'Twenty-five years … I am old I am/ old!'), echoing Svevo's second novel, *Senilità* ('Senility', 1898); passive, isolated and resigned ('Non vivo. Solo, gelido, in disparte'; 'I am not alive. Alone, stone-cold, set apart'); or inadequate and foolish ('scarso cervello, scarsa morale'; 'weak brain, weak morals'). Eugenio Montale, in his first collection of poems *Ossi di seppia* (1925), shuns the rhetoric of the poet as seer, probing instead his limits, his negative knowledge:

Non domandarci la formula che mondi possa aprirti,
sì qualche storta sillaba e secca come un ramo.
Codesto solo oggi possiamo dirti,
ciò che non siamo, ciò che non vogliamo.

('Non chiederci la parola')

(Don't ask us for the formula to open up new worlds for you,/ but
just some twisted syllables, dry as twigs./ This is all we can tell you
now,/ what we are not, what we do not want)

In the Sienese novelist Federigo Tozzi's 1919 work, *Con gli occhi
chiusi* ('With Eyes Closed'), the protagonist Pietro is depicted as
blind, deluded and passive, unable to see the violent, sordid reality
of the world around him, including in his supposedly pure loved
one, Ghisola, who ends up pregnant in a brothel. In 1921, Giuseppe Antonio Borgese, a critic and later anti-Fascist exile, published *Rubè*, a highly praised novel whose eponymous hero attempts
to combat his own passiveness and weakness by wilfully dedicating
himself to the interventionist cause of 1914-15 and then the Great
War. He fails to act decisively on any front, personal or political,
and comes to a miserable end.

The pattern is clear enough. Around the turn of the century, the
figure of the weak hero or antihero, a protagonist defined by the
very opposite of traditional, heroic virtues, came strongly to the
fore in Italian narrative. The antihero was passive, uncertain,
unknowing, unable to act or control his destiny, detached from the
world. The fall of the literary hero was one of the central developments of modern literature and it is worth looking at certain sources
which might explain the rise of the 'inetto' as a substitute.

One reason worth noting is reactive: this is precisely the phase
during which ideas of a strong self, even of a superhuman self (as
described by Nietzsche), of a strong nation, and a pure race, were
in circulation, waiting to be picked up and elaborated into something like an ideology by Fascism, and later Nazism. And indeed,
Gozzano, for one, was constantly mocking the trend for writers
such as d'Annunzio to flaunt Nietzschean ideas: here he is, ironi-

cally praising (and at the same time gently mocking) his simple 'Signora Felicita' in a poem of that name in *I colloqui* for not modishly following the latest Nietzschean trends (note the mocking rhymes with 'camicie' and 'felice'):

> Tu non fai versi. Tagli le camicie
> per tuo padre. Hai fatto la seconda
> classe, t'han detto che la Terra è tonda,
> ma tu non credi ... E non mediti Nietzsche ...
> Mi piaci. Mi faresti piú felice
> d'un'intellettuale gemebonda.

(You don't write verse. You cut shirts/ for your father. You did elementary/ school, they told you the Earth was round,/ but you don't believe it ... And you don't think about Nietzsche .../ I like you. You'd make me happier/ than would some moaning intellectual.)

Another source of the rise of the inept antihero lies in a theme central to this book: the disconcerting blows struck at the individual's sense of control and lucidity by modern mores: Svevo's heroes, like Gozzano's *alter egos*, live in the unremarkable, vacuous social milieux of the modern middle-classes. They are not laid low by grand sweeps of destiny but rather by the petty confusions, baffling complexities and social conventions which make up the obstacles of everyday life and against which they build odd, defensive worlds of their own, mired in introspection. Svevo's Zeno in *La coscienza di Zeno* (1923) is one of the great exemplars of the antihero's introspective hyper-elaboration: by mere accidents of timing (he spends too much time thinking when he should be acting), he distorts both the social world around him and his sense of will and of self. His marriage, his affairs, his business life are all determined by chance and neglect, often for the better. The chapter entitled 'Il fumo' ('Smoke') neatly illustrates the process, precisely because it centres on a struggle for self-control over an apparently meaningless activity of modern leisure, smoking. Zeno sets a date to give up, but finds that the pleasure of smoking the 'last cigarette' is so intense that he has to find ways of setting the date again (in all good faith) for the next last cigarette. And so, his addiction shifts and expands within his mind to include an addiction to finding anniversaries or significant patterns of numbers within dates to make them worthy of a last cigarette:

> Le date sulle pareti della mia stanza erano impresse coi colori piú varii ed anche ad olio. Il proponimento [to smoke my last cigarette], rifatto con la fede piú ingenua, trovava adeguata espressione nella forze del colore che doveva far impallidire quello dedicato al proponimento anteriore. Certe date erano da me preferite per la concordanza delle cifre. Del secolo passato ricordo una data che mi parve dovesse sigillare per sempre la bara in cui volevo mettere il mio vizio: 'Nono giorno del nono mese del 1899.' Significativa nevvero? Il secolo nuovo m'appartò della date ben altrimenti musicali: 'Primo giorno del primo mese del 1901.' Ancora mi pare che se quella data potesse ripetersi, io saprei iniziare una nuova vita.

> (The dates on the walls of my room were printed in the widest variety of colours, in oils too. Each new resolution [to smoke my last cigarette], made each time with the most innocent good faith, found its proper expression in the depth of the colour used, designed to put into the shade the colour marking the previous resolution. I tended to prefer certain dates because of a concordance in the figures. Before the end of the century, I remember one date which seemed particularly apt for sealing and burying once and for all my bad habit: 'The ninth day of the ninth month of 1899.' Strong stuff, wouldn't you say? And the new century brought me dates with quite a different kind of music to them: 'First day of the first month of 1901.' Still today, I feel that if only that date could be repeated, I would be able to begin a new life.)

By the end of this process, Zeno's fantasies and calculations loom larger than any real relationship between self, cigarette and the wider world: he is a sort of modern mystic or kabbalist for whom time operates on an another, cyclical scale: 'il tempo, per me, non è quella cosa impensabile che non s'arresta mai. Da me, solo da me, ritorna' (time, for me, is not that unthinking thing which never stops. For me, only for me, it returns).

Zeno's cigarette addiction begins with him stealing from his father, part of an explicitly 'Oedipal' dimension to his problems; Zeno replicates his addiction in his extra-marital affair in the novel (the pleasure of 'l'ultimo bacio' echoing the pleasure of 'l'ultima sigaretta'); and in any case, the image of the cigarette has clear sexual connotations in Freudian terms. All of which points to psychoanalysis and in particular, to the much-debated role of psychoanalysis in *La coscienza di Zeno*, as a final element to highlight the rise of the 'inetto' in modern literature.

Svevo's first contact with work by Freud, and with friends and relatives undergoing psychoanalysis, came around 1908, in the middle of the long fallow period between his second and third novels, and during the early period of his friendship with James Joyce. Although it would be wrong to say that Svevo became a convinced advocate of this new so-called 'science', *La coscienza di Zeno* uses some of the tools, language and ways of thinking of psychoanalysis to shape its unusual structure and to characterise its eccentric protagonist. The book is prompted by Zeno's analyst Dr S asking him to write down his memories, although Dr S famously warns that Zeno's account is a web of truth and lies (a distinction crucial for autobiographical or confessional literature, perhaps, but one that is secondary for psychoanalysis, since our lies about ourselves are as revealing as truths for Freud). Zeno's account includes dreams, jokes, slips and mistakes, tricks of language, neurotic obsessions and other recognisably Freudian elements (although their novelty was striking in early twentieth-century Italy). Dr S finally diagnoses an unresolved Oedipus complex, but Zeno rejects this, seeing himself as cured by the upturned world of the Great War (although it is doubtful that he is fully cured).

As well as displaying the wares of psychoanalysis, the novel also seems to satirise it, mocking Dr S and showing his work to have been both flawed and failed. More important still, however, is the way Zeno uses all this psychoanalytical paraphernalia to ask large questions about identity and to shape new literary means of exploring them. Perhaps the single, central theme of the book – the nature of and relationship between sickness and health – could not have emerged in all its complexities without the dimensions opened up by psychoanalysis. The non-linear timeline of the book, the constant doubt in the reader's mind as to what is true and what is not, the disproportionate shape of the chapters (smoking gets almost as much attention as the death of Zeno's father), the ironies and humour of the novel: all of these disruptive elements derive in some way from the inversions, counterintuitions and splits operated by psychoanalysis on our common perceptions of the self. And all of them showed the way for a century of complication and fragmentation (whether explicitly influenced by psychoanalysis or not) in the literary representation of the 'io'.

7.2. Doubles, masks, madness

Alongside the inept antihero, the first quarter of the century also saw the rise of other figures of the fragmented modern self. This section groups together three of them – the self as double, as mask and as insane – which reflect not so much the weakness as the indecipherable or hidden nature of identity; the self as enigma. The three sit particularly well together in a discussion of Italian literature of the period because they run like a seam through the work of a key modernist figure, Luigi Pirandello.

The figure of the doubled self, split into two opposing or mirroring halves, has been a staple of narrative since the myth of Narcissus or since the comedies of twins and disguise from classical theatre to Shakespeare to Goldoni. In the hands of the Romantic tradition of the nineteenth century, the double took a darker, more disquieting turn, as in the hugely influential *The Strange Case of Dr Jekyll and Mr Hyde* by Robert Louis Stevenson (1886). Stevenson is interested in the split between good and evil, but it is the pattern of doubling and the terrifying inner conflict of the self which makes the link from here to Freud's to modern split identity. In a far more playful, fable-like vein, Italo Calvino would take up Stevenson's theme in *Il visconte dimezzato* ('The Viscount Cut In Two', 1952), in which the knight Medardo is cloven in two by a cannonball during the crusades and emerges split into, precisely, his good half and his bad half. Calvino, however, is not interested in the anxiety of the split or the uncanny (to use a Freudian term) nature of the double; he rather uses the archetype as a comic and allegorical device (for a disguised critique of the Cold War, for example). Other doubles are to be found in the century's literature, from Ignazio Silone's *Pane e vino* (1936), whose Communist, anti-Fascist protagonist, Pietro Spina, lives disguised as a priest, to Pasolini's *Petrolio* (1992), whose vast ideological fresco of 1970s Italy is centred on Carlo split into his rational, cynical self and his sexually polymorphous, bodily self. But we need to return to Pirandello to find the most elaborate exploitation of the figure of the double in modern Italian literature.

It was in the nature of Pirandello's writing to rework a small number of philosophical and social themes obsessively. And perhaps the founding obsession of his work was the intuition that individuals are unknowable each to the other and to themselves. To make this impenetrability manifest, the doubling of an identity (again, social and/or philosophical) into two contradictory and yet simultaneous selves was one of his first and most geometrically neat tricks. Mattia Pascal is doubled up in his invented new self, Adriano Meis. In *Così è (se vi pare)* ('So It Is (If You Think So)', 1917), the plot revolves around contradictory versions of the local gossip about a certain 'signora Ponza': she is either signor Ponza's first wife or his second wife, or both. Even she herself cannot say, declaring at the play's end: 'Per me, io sono colei che mi si crede' (As far as I'm concerned, I am whoever people think I am). Here, doubling is only the first step in an explosive plurality of simultaneous identities within each of us, as every social situation or bond offers up a different version of the self; a notion Pirandello explored in his later novel, *Uno, nessuno e centomila* ('One, None and One-Hundred-Thousand', 1926).

Other situations of indeterminate identity abound in Pirandello's work, especially centred on bonds of family (see Chapter 5.3) and of sexual desire: a stepfather who almost becomes his daughter's lover (*Sei personaggi in cerca d'autore*, 'Six Characters in Search of an Author', 1921); a long-lost lover who has returned but may or may not be the person she claims to be (*Come tu mi vuoi*, 'As You Desire Me', 1930). Another archetypal form of doubling – where one character stands in or substitutes for another – is in evidence in *Il giuoco delle parti* ('The Game of Parts', or 'The Rules of the Game', 1918): the protagonist Leone Gala, cuckolded by his wife and lover and at risk of being killed in a duel through their machinations, uses the formal rules of duelling to force his wife's lover to stand in for him in the duel and so be killed in his stead. The substitution of lover for husband is, of course, a deeply ironic (or 'humoristic', in Pirandello's terms) turn, reflecting their parallel and opposing roles but reversing them. A further duality of identity is found in Pirandello's most famous work: in *Sei personaggi in cerca d'autore* the six 'fictional' characters (and the actors who play them) embody the contrasts and contradictions between fiction and reality, stage and auditorium, form and life, stasis and flux. Their identity is double, not because of a psychological split, but rather because they literally incarnate these larger conceptual dualities.

The mask was, if anything, even more central to Pirandello's work than the double: indeed, he famously entitled his published collected drama *Maschere nude* ('Naked Masks', various editions between 1918 and 1938). The image of the mask captures the fixed, surface of the self as presented to others, thin and provisional, rigid and fake, rooted in illusion and performance, and in conflict with our inner sense of self (itself, perhaps, another mask). Like the double, the mask derives from the most ancient traditions of theatre and ritual, but, again, Pirandello draws out of the tradition a very modern anxiety, which threatens to destabilise all sense of identity. All Pirandello's characters are forced to confront a moment of crisis, when the mask slips and the void of identity is revealed: most are forced swiftly to reconstitute a new mask, within and without, and to forget its nature. Only an odd and privileged few are able to contemplate life in full awareness of their subjection to the mask. The latter pay a high price of isolation and melancholy, however. This is Mattia Pascal's state at the end of his story: his insight, born of living and dying twice, leaves him like a ghost. The implication is that we are all as thin as phantasms beneath the surface of our provisional identities. In a more authentically tragic vein, Ersilia Drei, the protagonist of *Vestire gli ignudi* ('To Clothe the Naked', 1922), forced to confront the many masks (or clothes) imposed on her by a series of men (her employer, her lover, the writer who has rescued her), discovers that suicide is the only approximation to 'nakedness', to authenticity, open to her.

Finally, there is the category of madness. In Pirandello, as in much modernist literature, insanity represents more a philosophical rejection of the conventions of a society rather than a debilitating condition of mental sickness. It is another means for describing those ghost-like figures, those who have seen the void of identity and have refused to ignore it. The fullest exploration of the theme in Pirandello's *oeuvre* is *Enrico IV* ('Henry IV', 1922). Mocking the conventions of historical drama as well as the conventions of middle-class society, Pirandello imagines the court of Enrico as a sham, set up to appease the insane fantasies of a present-day, wealthy amnesiac, who wakes up after an accident believing he is Emperor Henry. In a typical inversion of roles, however, it emerges that 'Enrico' has woken up from his amnesia years before the stage-action begins; but has decided secretly to sustain the costumed illusion since it provides him with stability and with a clear perspective on the hypocrisies and fakeries of society around him. In this one, stunning shift of viewpoint, Enrico's power over his court has become real, and his subjects have become the fools, the unknowing actors of absurd roles (a neat definition of Pirandello's view of all of us). *Enrico IV* accelerates towards a tragic conclusion as the vortex of inversions of identity, power and perspective produces an explosion of repressed emotion and violence. The fact that this disaster has it roots in an ancient clash of jealousy and revenge (Enrico kills Belcredi, his rival for love from twenty years previously) underlines once more a distinctive characteristic of Pirandello's fragmentation of the self running through all three figures of the double, the mask and the mad: unlike the almost purely modern, ironic malaise of Svevo's antihero, Pirandello's notion of identity shows the most ancient myths and motifs reimagined as modern figures of the crisis in selfhood.

7.3. Memory

The third figure of the fragmentation of identity centres on the self split over time, through memory. This figure also has its roots in that crucial period of European modernism of the early twentieth century. Like the other two, its growth as a key feature of much modern literature is all but unimaginable without Freud, whose 'talking cure' was a process of accessing the repressed and often fictitious constructs of early memory. Thus, Svevo's Zeno attempts to reconstruct his own past through the unreliable and skewed resources of his own memory. But there is another seminal figure, from within French literature, who was at least as important as Freud in setting memory at the heart of modern literary imagination: Marcel Proust. Proust's monumental novel, *A la recherche du temps perdu* ('In Search of Lost Time', 1913-27) was hugely influential, in particular for its exploration of the erosions of self over time, contrasted with the patterns of 'involuntary' memory. Involuntary memory, for Proust, brought about a partial recovery of the forgotten past, of 'lost time', both through the spontaneous or unconscious stimuli of the senses (the famous dipped 'madeleine' cakes which provoke a cascade of childhood memories in his narrator) and through the aesthetics of a certain kind of artistic creation (such as *A la recherche* itself: the novel is, famously, structured as the story of its own genesis, circling around the narrator's memory).

In Italian literature, the influence of Proust ran parallel to a trend of lyrical, autobiographical writing in the group centred on *La Voce*. The latter produced a thread of fragmented, expressionistic prose and poetry, centred on the intense evocation of the remembered self, evident in works such as the Triestine Scipio Slataper's *Il mio Carso* ('My Carso', 1912). Both *La Voce* and Proustian influences are apparent in the role of memory in Eugenio Montale's second collection of poetry, *Le occasioni* ('Occasions', 1939). One of the most complex and successful poems of that collection is 'La casa dei doganieri' ('The Customs House', 1930), which is worth quoting in full here, for its swirling back and forth between the 'io' and the 'tu', the present and the past, physical and inner sensation, memory and forgetting:

Tu non ricordi la casa dei doganieri
sul rialzo a strapiombo sulla scogliera:
desolata t'attende dalla sera
in cui v'entrò lo sciame dei tuoi pensieri
e vi sostò irrequieto.

Libeccio sferza da anni le vecchie mura
e il suono del tuo riso non è piú lieto:
la bussola va impazzita all'avventura
e il calcolo dei dadi piú non torna.
Tu non ricordi; altro tempo frastorna
la tua memoria; un filo s'addipana.

Ne tengo ancora un capo; ma s'allontana
la casa e in cima al tetto la banderuola
affumicata gira senza pietà.
Ne tengo un capo; ma tu resti sola
né qui respiri nell'oscurità.

Oh l'orizzonte in fuga, dove s'accende
rara la luce della petroliera!
Il varco è qui? (Ripullula il frangente
ancora sulla balza che scoscende ...)
Tu non ricordi la casa di questa
mia sera. Ed io non so chi va e chi resta.

(You do not remember the customs house/ on the high, overhanging cliff:/ it waits for you, desolate, ever since the evening/ when the swarm of your thoughts entered there/ and stopped, restless.// A Libeccio wind has whipped its old walls for years/ and the sound of your laugh is no longer joyous:/ the compass spins crazily at random/ and the count of the dice does not add up./ You do not remember; another time drowns out/ your memory; a thread unravels.// I still have one end of it; but the house/ is moving away and on the rooftop the smoked/ weathervane turns without pity./ I still have one end of it; but you remain alone/ nor do you breathe here in the darkness.// Oh, fleeing horizon, where the rare/ light of the tanker burns!/ Is this the way through? (The surf still/ teems against the sheer crag ...)/ You do not remember the house of this/ evening of mine. And I do not know who is going and who is staying.)

A key dynamic of the poem is in the literal and figurative imagery of violence in the landscape and the weather (sheer cliff faces, swarms of restless thoughts, whipping winds, spinning compasses, deafening noise, bluster and darkness), capturing the sense of loss, isolation and disorientation created by the elusive processes of time and memory.

A broader, historical dimension to the poetics of memory and loss is found in two postwar writers, who were close to each other in their student days in 1930s Bologna and were both devotees of Proust: the novelist Giorgio Bassani and the poet Attilio Bertolucci. Bertolucci's poetry evokes the simple rhythms of provincial life in his native Romagna. In *La camera da letto* ('The Bedroom', 1984 and 1988), a long narrative poem telling the story of his family and his own life, this evocation is set against the often traumatic movements of history, and individual and collective memory, incorporating Proustian patterns of sensory perceptions and landscape seen as channels to the recovery of past time.

Bassani wrote a cycle of novels and short stories evoking the world of Ferrara in which he grew up (*Il romanzo di Ferrara*, 'The Novel of Ferrara', 1956-74), the most important of which was *Il giardino dei Finzi-Contini* (1962). Here, the autobiographical narrator recalls his unrequited first love for the aristocratic Micòl Finzi-Contini, together with the magical (and much idealised) world of the Finzi-Contini estate, contrasted with his own modest family and his Fascist father. This Jewish microcosm would all be swept to oblivion, as the novel makes clear from the outset, in a process begun by the Fascist Racial Laws of 1938 and culminating in the deportations to Nazi concentration camps, after the end of the novel. The entire Finzi-Contini family (aside from the already dead Alberto) would be murdered there. Memory, death and mourning pervade the novel, then, not only in the sense of retrospective doom but also in the strange obsessions with death, cemeteries and the past displayed by both Micòl and her father. At the same time, the novel sets these private patterns of memory against the steady march of public and civic history, as the novel also chronicles events in Ferrara, Italy and Europe as a whole in the interstices of the intimate central story (as Proust, towards the end of his novel, included the Great War within his unfolding narrative). And framing the entire novel is a present-day (i.e. 1950s) prologue, in which the adult narrator finds himself on an innocuous Sunday afternoon outing to some Etruscan tombs near Rome. Why, asks a young child in the car on the way, are we less sad about the Etruscan tombs than about more recent ones? Because they died so long ago, comes the answer, it is as if they had always been dead, had never lived. But, reflects the narrator, what does that tell us about the almost empty and forgotten family tomb of the Finzi-Contini? This thought prompts the memories which make up the bulk of the novel, but they also raise and leave hanging crucial issues surrounding memory: the play of presence, absence and affect in the movement between past and present, and the shadow of loss and death which hangs over all memory.

7.4. Identity destroyed

Il giardino dei Finzi-Contini, with its poignant tale of memory and mourning overshadowed by the Holocaust, makes for a useful transition to our last category of selfhood and its fragmentation in modern literature. Unlike the previous three, this category was born not of philosophical currents and their literary off-shoots (or not directly at least), but rather of the events – indeed of *the* central, catastrophic Event – of modernity. The wars of the modern age, the controlling power of the modern state (including the totalitarian state) and the nullifying, massifying trends of modern economics, culture and society, all seem to reach a devastating symbolic nadir in the Holocaust. The Nazi 'Final Solution to the Jewish Question' (and their parallel programmes of murder of gypsies, the mentally sick, political opponents and others) worked not only as a programme for the mass murder of millions, but also, prior to the slaughter, as systems for the dismantling or destruction of selfhood. Their victims, in other words, were dehumanised before being (and in order to be) killed as if they were subhuman. Literature, the literature of the Holocaust, has had to look for ways of representing this devastating fragmentation of identity also.

One Italian writer and one text stands out as of exceptional importance in this field, for Italy and for European literature as a whole: Primo Levi's *Se questo è un uomo* (1947; revised edition 1958). Having fought briefly in the Resistance, Levi was captured and deported to Auschwitz in February 1944. The Russians liberated the camp eleven months later in January 1945, and Levi began his long journey back home to Turin (recounted in his second book, *La tregua*, 'The Truce', 1963). Immediately, he began writing down stories about his experiences, and *Se questo è un uomo* was published by a small local publisher, De Silva, having been turned down by Einaudi and others.

Although Levi suggested that the book had been put together in a cathartic rush, and therefore without any great care or planning, it now appears as one of the most acute and lucid analyses and one of the most terrible evocations of the physical and psychological experience of the Holocaust victim (at least of those in the penultimate stages of degradation, since, as Levi pointed out in a later book, the real witnesses of the ultimate horror of the system were, by definition, no longer alive to tell their tale). And from the outset, from the very title of the book and the prefatory poem from which it is taken, Levi's central interest in the book is in the systematic destruction of human identity wrought by the Nazis:

> [...]
> Considerate se questo è un uomo
> Che lavora nel fango
> Che non conosce pace
> Che lotta per mezzo pane
> Che muore per un sí o per un no.
> Considerate se questa è una donna,
> Senza capelli e senza nome
> Senza piú forza di ricordare
> Vuoti gli occhi e freddo il grembo
> Come una rana d'inverno.
> [...]

(Consider if this is a man/ who works in the mud/ who knows no peace/ who fights for half a piece of bread/ who dies for a yes or a no./ Consider if this is a woman/ with no hair and no name/ with no strength to remember/ with empty eyes and a cold womb/ Like a toad in winter.)

The first three chapters of the book take us on a journey – in place, body and mind – from selfhood and normality (a world of choice, doubt and action, as Levi briefly describes his partisan days) to abjection and the voiding of the self. The stages he passes through each strip away some core element of identity. The train journey, the arrival, the initial selections for work or for immediate death, the showers, the shaving, the tattooing, the assignment to work, the deceptions and cruelties of other prisoners: each moment contains elements of loss of dignity, privacy, autonomy, individuality, solidarity and humanity. At each stage, Levi is especially alert to a residual sense of 'ordinary' humanity against which to judge the violence done to identity in the camps. Here, in the chapter 'Sul fondo' ('On the Bottom'), he defines the annihilation of identity precisely as the loss of habit, of the ordinary or everyday:

> [...] consideri ognuno, quanto valore, quanto significato è racchiuso anche nelle piú piccole nostre abitudini quotidiane, nei cento oggetti nostri che il piú umile mendicante possiede: un fazzoletto, una vecchia lettera, la fotografia di una persona cara. [...]
> Si immagini ora un uomo a cui, insieme con le persone amate, vengano tolti la sua casa, le sue abitudini, i suoi abiti, tutto infine, letteralmente tutto quanto possiede: sarà un uomo vuoto [...] Si comprenderà allora il duplice significato del termine 'Campo di annientamento.'

> ([...] each of you consider how much value and meaning there is in the smallest of our everyday habits, in the hundred objects that even the humblest beggar owns: a handkerchief, an old letter, the photo of a loved one [...]
> And now imagine a man who, along with his dearest, is deprived of his home, his habits, his clothes, in short of literally everything he possesses: he will be an empty shell of a man [...] And you will then understand the double meaning of the term 'Annihilation Camp'.)

The 'uomo vuoto' reaches an extreme form in the figure of the so-called 'Muselmann', the ghost-like prisoner who has lost all will to resist. And here, the abjection of identity is explicitly linked by Levi to his time, to modernity:

> [I Muselmänner] popolano la mia memoria della loro presenza senza volto, e se potessi racchiudere in una immagine tutto il male del nostro tempo, sceglierei questa immagine, che mi è familiare: un uomo scarno, dalla fronte china e dalle spalle curve, sul cui volto e nei cui occhi non si possa leggere traccia di pensiero.

> (They people my memory with their faceless presence, and if I wanted to capture in a single image all the evil of our time, I would choose this one, which I know so well: a bony figure of a man, his

forehead hanging low, his shoulders bent over, with not a trace of thought on his face or in his eyes.)

Even in the face of this, however, residues of 'ordinary' humanity, fragments of resistance, remain: Levi finds characters who have instincts and mechanisms for survival (and even the survival of a category such as character suggests resistance to the annihilation of all individual identity); he even finds figures of heroic altruism and companionship such as Lorenzo and Alberto, both in part responsible for his survival.

Here and throughout, through its probing of the extremes of the Holocaust, Levi's work offers subtle insights into the complexities of modern selfhood as explored in this chapter. The constant oscillation or struggle between forces of fragmentation and resistance – a battle all but lost from the outset in the concentration camps – is incessant and unresolved within the force fields of modern identity.

Selected reading

Marco Belpoliti, *Primo Levi* (Milan: Bruno Mondadori, 1997). A useful guide in dictionary format, from the same series as Cavaglion and Manotta below (see section 7.4 above).

Ann Caesar, *Characters and Authors in Luigi Pirandello* (Oxford: Oxford University Press, 1998) (7.2).

Joann Cannon, 'Memory and Testimony in Primo Levi and Giorgio Bassani', in Peter Bondanella and Andrea Ciccarelli (eds), *The Cambridge Companion to the Italian Novel* (Cambridge: Cambridge University Press, 2003), 125-35 (7.3).

Alberto Cavaglion, *Italo Svevo* (Milan: Bruno Mondadori, 2000). See entries on *La coscienza di Zeno*, 'Psicoanalisi' and others (7.1).

John Gatt-Rutter, *Italo Svevo. A Double Life* (Oxford: Oxford University Press, 1988). A rich personal and intellectual biography (7.1).

Robert Gordon, *Primo Levi's Ordinary Virtues: From Testimony to Ethics* (Oxford: Oxford University Press, 2001) (7.4).

Richard Klein, 'Zeno's Paradox', in *Cigarettes are Sublime* (London: Macmillan, 1993), 77-104. On Zeno's smoking (7.1).

Marco Manotta, *Luigi Pirandello* (Milan: Bruno Mondadori, 1998) (7.2).

Rebecca West, *Eugenio Montale: Poet on the Edge* (Cambridge, Mass.: Harvard University Press, 1981) (7.3).

8

Conclusion: Hybrid Forms

Rather than concluding by trying neatly to summarise a hugely varied century of literature and its complex relationship to modernity, I have chosen to use this final chapter to shift the perspective a little. Many of the previous chapters came at the literature-modernity bond 'from the outside in', moving from phenomena out there in the modern world (cities, wars, institutions, selves, etc.) in towards literature's responses to them. But the century also saw a vast array of changes *within* literature itself, *within* the very forms and patterns of the literary text, whatever its referential links to the outside world. This final chapter examines the formal revolutions of twentieth-century literature, not as a reflection of modernity but as a modern phenomenon in its own right. In doing so, it returns to some of the familiar key figures of previous chapters (e.g. the Futurists, Pirandello, Calvino), focuses for the first time in any detail on some others (e.g. Gadda), and moves towards suggesting a characterstic tone or mood in modern literature: a mood of ambiguity, complexity and irony.

The twentieth century was one of fervid and widespread formal experimentalism in literature. Attempts were made to overhaul every aspect of literary form, from language and style to genre and structure, to the very textual nature of literature. Poems were written comprising only two words or using cut-out shapes; novels were produced using clips from newspapers or transcriptions of recorded voices; stories appeared with no endings, characters or decipherable plot; and so on. And the effects of these extreme experiments were felt even in the most conventional literature. In particular, experimental literature was constantly blurring boundaries; between 'high' and 'low' culture, between registers of language, between genres and media, between literature and other forms of representation. In other words, it was constantly inventing and reinventing plural, multiple, hybrid literary forms. We can use this hybridity of form as a hook to hang our discussion on and as a token of the underlying patterns of modernity this book has been exploring. To understand its workings, we need first to locate its origins in the avant-garde (8.1), before moving on to see it at work in more formalist terms: first in literary language (8.2), then in genre (8.3) and, finally, in that elusive mood running through the century's literature (8.4).

8.1. Avant-gardes

Literary form was turned upside-down and inside-out in the most concerted and radical ways by the century's two key avant-garde literary movements, Futurism (1909 onwards) and the 'neo-avan-guardia' (1960s). Both movements emerged after intense periods of economic and socio-cultural modernisation in Italy (see Preface) and in moments of innovation and experiment throughout European culture; and for both, breaking down formal barriers and conventions was at the heart of their ideological and aesthetic projects.

Across all their richly varied and loud activity, the Futurists' aesthetic tools and principles remained remarkably constant, centred on forms of simultaneity, decomposition and dynamism as ways of transforming the world and our perception of it. All militated towards a process of explosive destruction followed by shifting recombinations of forms and processes; in other words, towards a principle and process of hybridisation. Early on in the movement's history, building on nineteenth-century innovations such as 'free verse', Marinetti and his group revolutionised poetic form by shattering it into a hybrid mix of collage, word-pictures, onomatopoeia, graphic shapes and lines (see the example in Chapter 4.1 of Marinetti's *'In the evening, lying on her bed, …'*). Marinetti's label for this audio-visual-textual hybrid was 'parola in libertà' ('word set free' or 'word in freedom'), inspired by 'immaginazione senza fili' ('wireless imagination'), as evoked in two key literary manifestoes of 1912 and 1913, *Manifesto tecnico della letteratura futurista* ('Technical Manifesto of Futurist Literature') and *Distruzione della sintassi – Immaginazione senza fili – Parole in libertà* ('Destruction of Syntax – Wireless Imagination – Words in Freedom'). In these, he unleashed an avalanche of subversive proposals, declaring the abolition of syntax, adjectives, adverbs, punctuation, all verb forms except for the infinitive, and even the 'io' itself. In place of these, he proposed noun-pairs and noun chains, linked by ever more outlandish analogies, the primacy of matter over meaning and its attributes sound, weight and noise. The aim was to dismantle stable categories of language, meaning and knowledge, and to replace them with the hybrid, intuitive energy of surprising combination and clashing associations.

The movement performed similar hybridising operations in many other spheres of activity and in many artistic forms other than poetry: its paintings (in the work of Balla, Boccioni and Carrà) broke down barriers of the frame, of pictorial time, of image and text; its theatre incorporated the performance of poetry and the graphics of its visual art; its music (in the work of Luigi Russolo) eschewed melody in favour of noise, performance, a transference between the senses (synaesthesia). Even the very manifestoes themselves were highly charged mixes of rhetoric, poetry, narrative and visuals. All these forms and forces came together in the famous Futurist 'serate' ('soirées'), held in theatres across Italy from 1913 onwards, which were vital and, on occasion, violent cocktails of declamation, music-hall, poetry, music, political polemic and simple provocation. Even in the movement's later, less strident phases (after the Great War and the rise of Fascism), when Futurism tended towards applied arts such as theatre- and costume-design, and towards forms growing out of new technologies such as radio or aeroplanes, the same underlying hybridising aesthetic principles still held sway.

Fifty years after Futurism was launched, a new avant-garde grouping emerged in Italy, known as the 'neo-avanguardia' (or 'Gruppo 63'). Certain elements transferred directly from one movement to the other – for example, the use of collage, or the general formalist impulse – but the tone and feel of the later movement was quite different, less aggressive and less bombastic, reflecting its decidedly leftist politics and the transformed cultural realities of the postwar world. The 'neo-avanguardia' was a loose grouping of young writers born in the 1930s. It originated in the late 1950s around a philosophical-cultural journal called *Il Verri* and a group of young poets looking to renew language in various ways (their first anthology was *I novissimi*, 'The Newest of the New', 1961). Over the course of the 1960s, it sponsored journals, anthologies, conferences and debates, as well as producing works of literature, before falling apart in the wake of the social unrest of 1968-9. Key figures, such as Edoardo Sanguineti, Nanni Balestrini, Umberto Eco, Giorgio Manganelli and Alberto Arbasino, shared a sense of the exhaustion of the socially committed realist writing dominant since the 1940s. They varied in their understanding of the functions of literature and literary forms: some were more politically radical, eventually feeding their ideas into the youth movements and political agitations of the late 1960s and 1970s (Balestrini); others were keen to open up the cultural sphere to mass culture (Eco); others still were devoted to a sophisticated linguistic experimentalism (Arbasino, Manganelli). All, however, retained the avant-garde belief in the radical implications of cross-fertilising, hybridising formal experiment as a way of transforming language and society.

As with Futurism, the 'neo-avanguardia''s achievements lay as much in conceptualising and intellectual sloganeering as in single, achieved works of art (perhaps because of the intrinsic dynamism of the avant-garde, as opposed to the static, monumental quality of the conventional work of art). And several of their guiding concepts and slogans, as well as their attempts at poetry and narrative, point us again towards hybridity. They equated form and language with ideology, and the subversion of the former meant the subversion of the latter. Meaning was plural, the text and its interpretations open processes (as Eco theorised in his influential work, *Opera aperta*, 'Open Work', 1962). Language, form, and indeed society were inherently split or schizoid, and the merest nudge was all that was needed to lay bare this division: Balestrini's phrase for this nudging of language was 'stuzzicare le parole', picking at or irritating words. This faith in subversion-from-within would lead many in the movement to work inside cultural industries of television and the modern media, seen as anathema to many other leftist intellectuals averse to mixing high with low. And, similarly, Eco and others would use the tools of high aesthetics (Eco's early work was on Thomas Aquinas and James Joyce) to analyse mass cultural products such as Superman or Snoopy comics.

As noted earlier and as for the Futurists, the 'neo-avanguardia' and its formalist and language-centred notions did not come out of a vacuum: they were influenced by a range of intellectual developments in Europe which were placing form, structure and the language at the very core of systems of knowledge and even human consciousness, and thereby shifting the boundaries of disciplines and categories. Trends such as structuralism (in linguistics, anthropology, psychoanalysis, political theory), object-driven narrative (such as in the French 'nouveau roman') and formalist cinema (in the work of Antonioni or the 'nouvelle vague') all fed into their experimentalism. For example, Sanguineti's novels *Capriccio italiano* ('Italian Fancy', 1963) and *Il gioco dell'oca* ('Snakes and Ladders', 1967) have much in common with the techniques of the 'nouveau roman'. The 'neo-avanguardia', then, was part of a larger vogue for formal experiment, and several writers contemporary to the movement, but either not part of it (Calvino) or openly hostile to it (Zanzotto), were taking comparable steps towards mixing forms within their texts around this time. The following sections will look more broadly at formal experiments in twentieth-century literature beyond the vanguards of Futurism and the 'neo-avanguardia'.

8.2. Literary languages

In Chapter 1 we looked at diversity of language as one of the founding characteristics of modern Italian literature. Aspects of this diversity feed directly into a discussion of formal experimentalism. Often, hybridity of form meant in practice a mixing of levels and types of language, whether through the intermingling of registers, idioms and languages, through the mixing of oral and written language, or through the use of raw, unfinished, or simply ugly forms of language.

We can see a general promiscuous multilingualism – the strident juxtaposition in single works, even in single sentences, of terms from different languages, dialects, registers, idioms – at work as a vital resource for modern Italian literature around the 1950s and 1960s especially. The 'neo-avaguardia' poet Edoardo Sanguineti happily mixed Italian with Latin, Greek and exclamatory noises, starting with his first work *Laborintus* (1956). The Resistance writer Beppe Fenoglio, enamoured of the adventure stories of English literature, mixed his Italian with an eccentric mock-English quite unique to his work. The trilingual poet Amelia Rosselli wrote variously and often interchangeably in Italian, French and English. By far the most significant and sophisticated (and influential) model for this multilingualism, however, was the work of Carlo Emilio Gadda.

Gadda's work is notoriously difficult to grasp, because of its philosophical and linguistic complexity, and because of its scabrously pessimistic vision of the world and our capacity to grasp it. In fact, these two axes of complexity and pessimism are deeply interconnected: the labyrinthine, chaotic, web-like qualities of Gadda's universe, prone to decay and devoid of transparency, resisting all representation or synthesis, are reflected in a language which is polyphonic, baroque, hybrid or 'plurilinguistic' (the term chosen by the most influential contemporary analyst of Gadda's work, Gianfranco Contini). Gadda's languages create a sense of excess and obsession, a sense of neurosis in the relationship of language to the world (in human civilisation, in the modern world in particular and, more narrowly still, in the version of modernity incarnated in Fascism).

Gadda's two principal works of fiction, *La cognizione del dolore* (1938-41 in serial form; republished 1963) and *Quer pasticciaccio brutto de via Merulana* (1946; republished 1957), are packed with different levels and types of language, often within the same paragraph or sentence. In the mix are standard Italian, archaic Italian, foreign terms (French, Latin, Spanish, German etc.), technical and philosophical jargon, and dialects (in *Quer pasticcaccio brutto de via Merulana*, for example, there is Roman, Neapolitan, Tuscan, Molisean, and others). Here is one extract, from the later book, in which a suspected child rapist and murderer (Pirroficoni) is arrested and beaten:

Il mal capitato Pirroficoni fu ridotto in fin di vita a bussa da un taliana di quelli: perché gli si voleva estorcere ad ogni modo, in 'camera di sicurezza', la veridica ammissione d'aver istuprato certe bimbe. Paracadde giù da' nuvoli e implorava che no, che non è vero un corno: ma ne buscò da stiantare. Oh mani generosi del Beccaria!

L'Urbe, proprio al tempo de' suoi accessi di buon costume e di questurinnizzata federzonite, l'ebbe a conoscere (1926-27) alcuni periodici strangolamenti di bambine: e ne reliquavano alle prata e le spoglie e lo strazio, e la misera e spenta innocenza: là, là extra muros, dopo le divozioni suburbicarie, e l'epigrafi degli antichi marmi e sacelli. *Consule Federsonio, Rosamaltonio enixa: Maledito Merdonio dictatore impestatissimo.* Il Ficconi Pirro, meschino!, dameggaiva in allora una sua dama anzichenò butirrosa comeché stagionatuzza, ma di alquanto impedita accessione: quinto piano: casamento umbertino; portiere un sul portone; marito presente, efficiente ... in pantofole: grappoli di coinquilini ad libitum, glossatori de natura, più che Irnerio.

(The hapless Pirroficoni was beaten within an inch of his life by a motley gang, in the 'high security room', to get out of him, any which way, the truthful confession of having raped some little baby girls. His astonishment was total, dumbfounded, an' he begged and pleaded no, it was stuff and nonsense: but he got 'imself done over all the same. O, for the caring *manes* of Beccaria!

The Urbs of Rome – caught up in one of its drives for civic decency, its cops down with a bad case of federzonitis – was confronted (1926-27) with a number of intermittent stranglings of young girls. They lay in rest, out there in the meadows, their bodily remains and their terrible suffering, and their wretched, snuffed-out innocence: there, out there, extra muros, after the suburbicarian shrines and the epigraphs of the ancient marble tombstones and altars. *Consule Federsonio, Rosamaltonio enixa: Maledito Merdonio dictatore impestatissimo.* Ficconi Pirro, meanwhile – the poor fool! – was at that moment courting his courtesan, who was more lardy than other-wise, not to say a little past her sell-by date, but also somewhat tricky to find: fifth floor, turn-of-the-century block, porter on the look out at the door, husband who knew what he was doing, ready and waiting ... in his slippers, and knots of tenants ad libitum, natural born glossators of the situation, like so many Saint Irneriuses.)

Gadda's cacophony of languages rings in the reader's head, and the grim 'tabloid' scenario behind it all – the sordid murder of young girls – struggles to emerge. The novel, as the Russian critic Mikhail Bakhtin argued, is here played out as a carnivalesque mix of voices. This is even more evident in an aspect of modern literature already noted in Chapter 1.2: the use of oral, colloquial language. This trend – apparent in a large number of writers, from Palazzeschi to Pasolini, from Celati to Tondelli – can in part be ascribed to the strong realist line running through the century's literature, since to transcribe spoken language is to capture the plurality of voices, the soundtrack of the real world, rather than to describe it or to evoke it. But it also – and often, simultaneously – tends to produce a textual quality and rhythm, a consonance and/or dissonance in the prose, which makes it formally experi-mental, disturbing the qualities of literary expression. The following two examples, from Palazzeschi and Tondelli, show in their different ways how pure orality can seem oddly rhythmic and powerful:

–Noi tutte siamo tanto lusingate, non è vero mie care?
–Tanto!
–Tutte!
–Molto!
–Infinitamente.
–Già!
–Sí!
–Ma davvero!
–E come!
–Siamo tanto lusingate di accogliere, signor Perelà …

Palazzeschi, Il codice di Perelà, 1911

('We're all so flattered, aren't we my dears?'
'So much!'
'All of us!'
'Greatly!'
'Extremely'
'Indeed!'
'Yes!'
'Really very!'
'I'd say!'
'We're so flattered to welcome signor Perelà …')

[…] 'Ma che fai, sei pazzo?'
    'Taci, imbecille, taci!', grida 'Vattene via, prepara la siringa'. Liza si fa sulla porta, sbotta in un Oooooohhhhh e una bestemmia. 'Stai alla porta cazzo' sbraita Rino 'se entra qualcuno siamo fregati tutti!'

Tondelli, Altri libertini, 1980

('What are you doing, you must be mad!'. 'Shut up you idiot, shut up', she shouts 'Get out and do the syringe.' Liza shoots up at the door, bursts out with an 'Aaaaahhh' and a round of swearing. 'Stay by the door, fuck it', Rino barks, 'if anyone comes in here, we're all in the shit!')

To mix literary language with the banal language of everyday speech is to chip away at the specificity and privilege of literature, what sets it apart as 'high' culture. The third form of hybridisation of language takes this process further still, challenging the very notion of literature as an aesthetic form. Most conceptions of literature agree that it should aspire to beauty, to a use of language defined variously as elegant, refined, harmonious, balanced, regular, shaped, controlled, and so on. Of course, these values vary over time and writers who challenge them are commonly criticised for failing to stick to the canons of beauty, only to be hailed as aesthetically triumphant later on. Nevertheless, it is extraordinary and exceptional to see in the twentieth century certain writers openly aspiring to forms of language which are studiedly unrefined, unfinished, even ugly.

Marinetti was the first to declare 'Facciamo coraggiosamente il "brutto" in letteratura' (1912) ('Let's have the courage to make "ugly" literature'); and something of this anti-aestheticism is to be found in Luigi Russolo's dissonant art of noise, for example, as it is at the end of the century in the 'cannibali', with their blood-splattered indifference and flat delivery. Two later writers who invested systematically and subtly in forms of incompleteness were Gadda, almost all of whose texts were left incomplete in some way (although rarely 'ugly'), reflecting a philosophical conception of the disintegration of knowledge; and then Pasolini, particularly in the final years of his life (the early 1970s), when he more and more frequently left his literary work in a state of temporary, disordered, unfinished and unpolished suspension. The two key examples from this period are his poetry collection, *Trasumanar e organizzar* ('To Transcend the Human, To Organise', 1971), and his unfinished novel, *Petrolio* (1992). The latter, even in its finished form, was designed to seem incomplete, a chaos of textual notes, comments and lacunae. The first page in the published version – 'Note number 1', as it is called – contains a single footnote on an otherwise blank page: 'This novel has no beginning'. *Trasumanar e organizzar* is full of long, rambling, irregular pieces, many using political jargon or highly prosaic analytical language, whose over-extended lines struggle to acquire the shape and rhythm one would expect of poetry. This is raw poetry, made deliberately ugly in order to put on display the desecration of aesthetic form.

8.3. Genres

Every era produces new forms and new genres for literature, typically made up of hybrids of older genres; and the twentieth century was no exception. But more than simply adding new genres (for example, the genre of testimony, as we saw in chapters 4 and 6), the twentieth century saw a dramatic process of deregulation, when many conventions of form and genre fell away entirely (at least apparently). In their place, an organic conception of the relationship of form to content – in which every work shaped itself according to its own peculiar demands and nature, not according to prescribed rules – came to dominate. This was perhaps most evident in lyric poetry in which, ever since Leopardi in the early nineteenth century, rules of prosody had stretched and loosened, until free verse and even looser forms such as prose poetry (for example, in Dino Campana's visionary poem cycle, *Canti orfici*, 'Orphic Songs', 1914) became the norm. Even free verse, however, was rarely completely free from norms of metre and rhyme, except in extreme cases such as the Futurist 'parole in libertà'. Hidden metrics and hints at rhyme (in the form of assonance and alliteration) fed themselves into even the most apparently free writing. Thus, Ungaretti's fragmentary lines often contained veiled or split instances of standard verse. His boldest experiment in brevity, the poem 'Mattino' ('Morning') in *L'allegria* – which reads in its entirety 'M'illumino / d'immenso' ('I am lit up / in immensity') – is in reality a standard 'settenario' (7-syllable line) split in two. Thus, innovation in form and genre was constantly in tension with convention and tradition, and new forms were often more self-conscious and less organic than they might at first have seemed.

The modern novel in Italy showed a striking propensity to mix and match and reinvent its genres. This was perhaps because of an ambiguity in origin, with elements of the nineteenth-century European novel tradition mixing with the influence of the longer-standing Italian 'novella' tradition, stretching back to Boccaccio. Whatever the reason, modern hybrid genres are not hard to find. For example, Pirandello (much to the disapproval of Croce, with his purist conception of literary form) imported philosophy into his fiction and theatre, setting the flow of character and situation alongside conceptual analysis of issues of identity and destiny. In *Uno, nessuno e centomila*, the fragmented, ironic and multi-layered form of the novel reflects both the unhinged character of the protagonist, Vitangelo Moscarda, and the vertiginous plurality of human identity illustrated by his predicament. The resultant novel might be categorised as a 'philosophical novel', a term we could loosely apply also to Gadda's *La cognizione del dolore* (1963), Calvino's *Palomar* (1983) and many others.

The hybrid aspect of the modern novel can also be traced back to the one great novel of nineteenth-century Italy, Manzoni's *I promessi sposi*, itself something of a hybrid in its mix of fact and fiction, of narrative and historical analysis (as well as political, theological and legal analysis), and of conventions of realism, fable, romantic fiction, the gothic tale, Sternian digression and irony. Although highly conservative and moralistic in many aspects, Manzoni's novel left a flexible legacy in formal terms. For example, in his use of narrative as a mode of enquiry into history (seen even more clearly in Manzoni's brief appendix to his novel, *Storia della colonna infame*, 'History of the Column of Infamy', 1842), he was a model for twentieth-century writers and also historians, such as Leonardo Sciascia and Carlo Ginzburg. Sciascia wrote several so-called 'romanzi d'inchiesta' ('enquiry novels'), mixing reflections, memories, stories and analyses with archives, facts and material traces of historical events. For example, *Morte dell'inquisitore* (1964) tells the story of the only man ever to kill an Inquisitor in Sicily, using graffiti on prison walls, archival documents from Sicily and Spain, previous legendary and official historical accounts; and

L'affaire Moro (1978) analyses the kidnapping and murder of Aldo Moro by way of letters, codes, clues, tricks, rituals and literary precedents. The form of the 'inchiesta' which Sciascia invents here (or reinvents, with a debt to Manzoni) finds echoes in the narrative microhistories of Carlo Ginzburg (e.g. *I formaggi e i vermi*, 'The Cheese and the Worms', 1976), who, like Sciascia, later adapted his methods to analyse the 'hidden history' of Italy's recent terrorist years, in *Il giudice e lo storico* ('The Judge and the Historian', 1991).

If hybrids of narrative and history or memory and history were one means to generic innovation in the novel, another was to mix 'high' and 'low' or elite and popular cultural forms. Some of the strongest influences on the twentieth-century Italian novel have been popular nineteenth-century literary genres such as adventure stories (e.g. Robert Louis Stevenson, Emilio Salgari), children's literature (e.g. the immensely popular *Pinocchio* by Carlo Collodi, 1883, and *Cuore*, 'Heart', by Edmondo De Amicis, 1886) or historical epics (e.g. Dumas). Undoubtedly the richest example, however, of such a symbiosis between high and low has been the detective novel or the 'giallo' (after the yellow-covered Mondadori series of the 1930s). Three key examples, from the second half of the century, show the various literary uses to which the 'giallo' form has been put. First, Gadda's *Quer pasticciaccio brutto de via Merulana* uses the investigation by Francesco 'don Ciccio' Ingravallo of the murder of a wealthy woman in Rome as the hook on which to hang its philosophical investigations (on evil, on the nature of knowledge), its linguistic experiments and its satire. Secondly, Sciascia famously made use of the 'giallo' form in novels such as *Il giorno della civetta* ('The Day of the Owl', 1961) and *A ciascuno il suo* ('Each to His Own', 1966) to become the first writer to confront the mechanisms and pervasive power of the Sicilian mafia. Both Gadda and Sciascia make a point of undermining the closure of the traditional detective story, leaving murders unsolved and the detective baffled. Finally, Umberto Eco's *Il nome della rosa* (1980) uses the detective novel genre with much postmodern formal trickery and witty nods to the tradition (the detective is called 'Guglielmo da Baskerville', in an obvious echo of Conan Doyle's *Hound of the Baskervilles*). As with Gadda, the genre is a hook on which to hang philosophical reflections, here on semiotics, the nature of laughter and medieval theology. Unlike Gadda and Sciascia, however, Eco retained as many features of the classic detective novel as he could (series of murders, a brilliant detective with naïve assistant, a closed number of suspects, secret codes, and so on), playing up the pleasures of the genre, although he too in the end shows his detective to have been something of a fool. And it is perhaps no coincidence that, after the massive success of *Il nome della rosa* (and others such as Carlo Fruttero and Franco Lucentini, and Giorgio Scerbanenco), later years of the century saw the 'giallo' grow in popularity in both high-brow and low-brow fiction. Younger authors such as Carlo Lucarelli (*Almost Blue*, 1997) came to prominence, basing their work in fiction but also in 'true crime' narrative which touched on occasion politically sensitive crimes of recent Italian history. The greatest publishing phenomenon of the 1990s, however, was Andrea Camilleri, whose Sicilian detective novels and stories about Inspector Montalbano were tightly executed and immensely successful genre products, with enough touches of the flavours (the cooking, especially) and the language of Sicily to echo distantly the world of Verga and the Sicilian literary tradition.

The collapse of distinction between literary and popular culture evident in the evolution of the 'giallo' points us in one further direction for our discussion of the hybridisation of genre, that is the mixing of literary form with an eclectic variety of input from other media altogether. The Futurists, again, set the standard, drawing on the aesthetics of music hall, taking its fragmented, interactive, improvised, and transgressive nature as a model for its own theatre (see the manifesto, *Il teatro di varietà*, 'Music Hall Theatre', 1913), just as the language of television and advertising would infiltrate the young 'cannibali' writers of the 1990s. Comics or 'fumetti' grew as a popular medium in the 1930s (as with the 'giallo', the key player was the publisher Mondadori, with its Mickey Mouse, or 'Topolino' stories) and were eventually accepted by the intellectual caste as a 'serious' cultural form, under the influence of figures such as Fellini, Umberto Eco and Oreste del Buono. The film screenplay, a form practised by many writers (as we saw in Chapter 1.3.1), took on the features of a new genre, poised between pen and screen, as Pasolini argued in an important essay of 1965. Finally, even the very tools of writing, which evolved over the course of the century from pen to typewriter to word processor, had their impact on form, as seen in Eco's use of extracts from computer files in his second novel, *Il pendolo di Foucault* (1988).

8.4. Irony, fantasy, comedy, play

Formal experiment and the hybridisation of language and genre contributed to creating a mood or tone which ran through a great deal of twentieth-century literature, and which is perhaps its single most characteristic feature. It fed a mood of doubt, uncertainty or instability and a tone of ambivalence or irony. Our final task is to tap into this modern literature of doubt.

Experimentalism, from its modernist through to its postmodernist incarnations, was rooted in a deep scepticism about tradition and knowledge, about complete and stable forms, about single and lucid meanings in language. As a result, it used form, language, indeed literature itself ironically, self-consciously aware of its own limits and uncertainties. Pirandello set this doubting, ironic mood for Italian literature in his influential essay of 1908, *L'umorismo* ('Humour' or 'Humorism'). Close to irony, Pirandello's 'humorism' is a form of humour in which broad comedy (built on the perception of a discrepancy, 'l'avvertimento del contrario') is shot through with tragicomic pathos for the situation felt behind the comedy ('il sentimento del contrario'). And the figure of the 'umorista' is a particular kind of writer (Manzoni is again a model here, as are Cervantes and others), sensitive to the complexities of the discrepancies which litter the world and the simultaneous, tragicomic contradictory realities to be found there. The humorist is, for

Pirandello, perplexed by the world, and his/her writing and reading captures this mood of perplexity.

Forms of ironic humour feature strongly in other key writers in tune with modernism, such as Italo Svevo or Guido Gozzano. Variants of it spread in several different experimental directions in the early decades of the century. The fantastic literature of this period – by writers such as Massimo Bontempelli (practitioner of so-called 'realismo magico'), Alberto Savinio (a 'metaphysical' artist, like his brother, the painter Giorgio de Chirico) and Tommaso Landolfi – used humour as a tool for surprising and disquieting the reader and dismantling the coordinates of rational, knowable reality. Similarly, the movement in theatre known as the 'theatre of the grotesque' (whose main practitioners were Luigi Chiarelli, Luigi Antonelli and Enrico Cavacchioli) used a dark, disturbing humour to uncover its vision of the grotesque anomalies in society. And a vein of violently grotesque humour, satire and parody dominates the devastating, degraded worldview of Gadda, in his novels and other works.

Another vein of humour, this time of a broader comic kind, had its source in aspects of the Futurist movement. Futurist theatre drew on facile, quickfire forms of comedy, echoing music hall rhythms; many of its short plays ('sintesi') were little more than staged jokes. More importantly perhaps, bombastic comedy was integral to the rhetoric of the Futurist manifesto, which was so crucial in determining the impact and direction of the movement. The tone was set by Marinetti but aped by many other practitioners. For example, the French writer Guillaume Apollinaire penned a manifesto in French, 'L'Antitradition futuriste' ('Futurist Antitradition', 1914) which divided the world into lists of the good and the bad, sending out 'roses to …' the former and 'shit to …' the latter. The brief, sketch-like jokes of the Futurists influenced also the most celebrated comic writer of the interwar years, Achille Campanile, whose absurdist humour focused on the stupidity of the world around him, and made much of its formal reductiveness (e.g. *Tragedie in due battute*, 'Two-Line Tragedies', 1924).

A more complex 'comic' product of the Futurist movement was the 1914 manifesto 'Il controdolore' ('Counterpain'), by Aldo Palazzeschi, who allied himself temporarily to the Futurists after 1909. 'Il controdolore' is a little less syncopated and strident than most of the movement's manifestos, calling for something like a moral and aesthetic revolution to upturn everything grey, serious, painful and heavy about the world, through the instrument of laughter:

Noi futuristi vogliamo guarire le razze latine, e special-
mente la nostra, dal dolore cosciente, lue passatista [...
vogliamo] 1. **Distruggere il fantasma** romantico ossessionante
e doloroso **delle cose** dette **gravi**, estraendone e sviluppandone il
ridicolo [...] 4. **Invece di fermarsi nel buio del dolore,**
attraversarlo con slancio, per entrare nella luca della
risata. [...] 8. Trasformare gli ospedali in ritrovi divertenti, medi-
ante five o'clock thés esilarantissimi, café-chantants, clowns. [...]
12. Trasformare i manicomi in scuole di perfezionamento per le
nuove generazioni.

(We Futurists want to cure the Latin races, and especially our own,
from our waking pain, that passéiste pox [... we want] 1. To destroy
the obsessive and painful Romantic ghost of so-called weighty
things, extracting from them and developing their laughable side
[...] 4. Instead of staying in the dark of pain, to cut through it with
force and move into the light of laughter. [...] 8. To transform
hospitals into fun places, with exhilarating five o'clock teas, café-
chantants, clowns. [...] 12. To turn mental asylums into finishing
schools for the new generations.)

The lightness of touch and laughter proposed here were already in place in Palazzeschi's novel *Il codice di Perelà*, and are full of pointers to later forms of modern comedy, whether grotesque or absurd, modernist or postmodernist. Indeed, if we jump forward to the 1970s, and to what can loosely be labelled a postmodernist moment, threads of connection can be drawn to modernist moods of irony, fantasy and comedy. The fantastic and elements of the

grotesque persisted in a strong line of later narrative, most emble-
matically in the work of Anna Maria Ortese, who first wrote under
the tutelage of Bontempelli in the 1930s but emerged as a central
figure only in the 1980s. Ortese and younger writers such as Paola
Capriolo used elements of disquieting irony, surprise and strange
humour to create their fantastic moods and their elusive forms.
Another line of fantasy writing was found in science-fiction: Stefano Benni mixed fantasy with elements of surreal, linguistic
experiment and humour to create a highly successful new genre of
comic futuristic novels such as *Baol* (1990). Of course, science,
fantasy and humour had already been merged in Calvino's 1960s
inventions, *Le cosmicomiche* ('Cosmicomics', 1965) and *Ti con zero* ('T
Zero', 1968). And in Calvino Palazzeschi's rebellion against 'le cose
gravi' found a crucial late twentieth-century champion: one of late
lectures in *Lezioni americane* ('American Lessons', subtitled 'Six Proposals for the Next Millennium', 1988), was, precisely, a
celebration of 'Leggerezza' ('Lightness').

The figure of Calvino, as so often, is crucial here. As well as
offering connections back to modernist scepticism and humour or
fantasy, his work also demonstrates the distinct game-playing or
ludic quality of the postmodern moment, with its pure, combinato-
rial play of language, surface and form, and the use of pastiche.
Much of his work of the 1970s could be taken to illustrate the point,
but the importance of the 1979 work *Se una notte d'inverno un viaggiatore* in particular cannot be overstated. In it, Calvino plays endless
narrative and formal games with multiple levels of reading, writing,
publishing, translating and the chaos of meanings and desires these
practices provoke. The protagonist is 'You', the reader of the book,
and the work is structured as a search for the book 'You' are
reading, a search constantly interrupted, as the elusive book is
continually blocked after different versions of its first chapter.
Although Calvino has much to say here about language, meaning,
and literary style, *Se una notte d'inverno un viaggiatore* is above all an
exercise in what the French thinker Roland Barthes would call the
'erotics' of the text; that is, the alternately teasing, beguiling, frus-

trating, partly fulfilled and always deferred pleasures of reading. The analogy is made explicit by Calvino at one point, when (the male) 'You' finally succeed in having sex with Ludmilla, the female reader and object-of-desire within the text.

Other texts of this period showed the same playful dismantling and fragmenting of textual form as seen in *Se una notte d'inverno un viaggiatore*, in ways that perhaps ultimately suggest a deep-seated ambivalence and instability in the very notion of literature itself. One of the most intellectually brilliant and creative figures of the 'neo-avanguardia' of the previous decade, Giorgio Manganelli, had made much of the formal play of literature and language, and the comic potential of this play (an early book was entitled *Hilaro-tragoedia*, 1964). Manganelli's play was more sceptical and darker than Calvino's, however, based on a conception of literature as artifice and concealment (another of his books was called *La lettera-tura come menzogna*, 'Literature As Lies', 1967). As a result, Manganelli shows more of the deep scepticism, even nihilism, of postmodernism than Calvino, with its sense of the collapse of history and other grand discourses such as truth, value and language (and so also literature) into simulation or fakery. In the same year as *Se una notte d'inverno un viaggiatore* (and within months of the appearance of Eco's *Il nome della rosa*), Manganelli published *Cen-turia*, a short sequence of a hundred 'novels', each only a page long, each a pastiche of a certain type of novel (as were each of Calvino's mock novel-openings in alternate chapters of *Se una notte d'inverno un viaggiatore*). Like Calvino in the famous first pages of that book ('You are about to start reading Italo Calvino's new novel, *If on a Winter's Night a Traveller*. Relax. Gather your thoughts. Stop thinking of anything else [...]'), Manganelli opens his book with an attempt to tell his reader how to read the book. In Mangan-elli's case, however, this postmodern play with the reader takes a grotesque, allegorical turn, which seems to speak not of Calv-ino's never-ending spiral of narrative pleasure, but, if anything, of the death of literature:

Se mi si consente un suggerimento, il modo ottimo per leggere questo libercolo, ma costoso, sarebbe: acquistare diritto d'uso d'un grattacielo che abbia il medesimo numero di piani delle righe del testo da leggere; a ciascun piano collocare un lettore con il libro in mano; a ciascun lettore si dia una riga; ad un segnale, il Lettore Supremo comincerà a precipitare dal sommo dell'edificio, a man mano che transiterà di fronte alle finestre, il lettore di ciascun piano leggerà la riga destinatagli, a voce forte e chiara. E' necessario che il numero delle piani corrisponda a quello delle righe, e che non via siano equivoci tra ammezzato e primo piano, che potrebbero causare un imbarazzante silenzio prima dallo schianto.

(If I may be allowed to make a suggestion, the best, although also the costliest, way to read this little book would be: first acquire access to a skyscraper which has the same number of floors as the book has lines; place a reader on each floor, book in hand; give each reader a line; at an agreed signal, the Supreme Reader will launch himself from the top of the building, and as he gradually passes by in front of the windows, the reader on each floor will read out his chosen line, in a strong clear voice. The number of floors must be the same as the number of lines and there must be no ambiguity between the first floor and the mezzanine, which might cause an embarrassing silence just before the crash.)

This is not quite, however, the 'apocalyptic' scenario we encountered earlier in Chapter 2.1, for example in the devastating finale of Svevo's *La coscienza di Zeno*. The death plunge in *Centuria* is a beginning not an ending; a prelude to the darkly ambivalent but multiple pleasures and risks of a literature of modernity.

Selected reading

Manuela Bertone and Robert Dombroski (eds), *Carlo Emilio Gadda. Contemporary Perspectives* (Toronto: Toronto University Press 2000) (see section 8.2 above).

Joann Cannon, *Postmodern Italian Fiction: The Crisis of Reason in Calvino, Eco, Sciascia, Malerba* (London: Associated University Presses, 1989) (8.4).

Remo Ceserani, *Raccontare il postmoderno* (Turin: Bollati Boringhieri, 1997) (8.4).

Edinburgh Journal of Gadda Studies at http://www.arts.ed.ac.uk/italian/gadda/ An excellent online resource about Gadda (8.2).

Joseph Farrell, *Leonardo Sciascia* (Edinburgh: Edinburgh University Press, 1995) (8.3).

Robert Gordon, 'Rhetoric and Irony in Pasolini's Late Poetry', in Peter Hainsworth and Emanuela Tandello (eds), *Italian Poetry Since 1956*, supplement to *The Italianist* (15) (1995), 138-55. An attempt to analyse Pasolini's later 'ugly' poetry (8.2).

Anne Mullen and Emer O'Beirne (eds), *Crime Scenes: Detective Narratives in European Culture since 1945* (Amsterdam: Rodopi, 2000). Several chapters on Italian writers (8.3).

Antonio Pagliaro (ed.), *Il giallo*, special issue of *Spunti e ricerche* 16 (2001). Essays on recent Italian detective fiction (Scerbanenco, Lucarelli, Camillaeri) (8.3).

Christopher Wagstaff, 'The Neo-avantgarde', in Michael Caesar and Peter Hainsworth (eds), *Writers and Society in Contemporary Italy* (Leamington Spa: Berg, 1984), 35-62 (8.1).

John White, *Literary Futurism* (Oxford: Oxford University Press, 1990). Very full discussion of formal innovations in Futurist work (8.1).

Glossary of Writers

Aleramo, Sibilla (1876-1950) (pseud. Rina Faccio). Author of an important autobiographical novel about the condition of women, *Una donna* (1906); also diarist and close to many literary intellectuals of the early part of the century.

Alvaro, Corrado (1895-1956). Novelist, in a realist vein, especially associated with his native South; best-known work, *Gente in Aspromonte* (1930).

Ammaniti, Niccolò (1966-). Included in the *Gioventù cannibale* anthology (1996); has gone on to write taut, successful novels such as *Io non ho paura* (2001).

Arbasino, Alberto (1930-). Experimental novelist, sophisticated satirical and cultural journalist, travel writer; among the founders of 'Gruppo 63'; major works, often later republished in revised editions, include *Fratelli d'Italia* (1963), *Super-Eliogabalo* (1969), *Un paese senza* (1980).

Bacchelli, Riccardo (1891-1985). Novelist and major literary figure of the Fascist years; worked in several genres, including the historical novel and the family saga (*Il mulino del Po*, 1938-40).

Balestrini, Nanni (1935-). Experimental and politically radical poet and novelist (e.g. *Vogliamo tutto*, 1971); associated with 'neo-avanguardia' of 1960s and leftist groups of 1970s such as 'Potere Operaio'.

Ballestra, Silvia (1969-). Young novelist and short-story writer; first published in Tondelli's *Under 25* anthology in 1985; sharply ironic novels include *Gli orsi* (1994).

Banti, Anna (1895-1985) (pseud. Lucia Lopresti). Novelist and co-editor (with her husband, art historian Roberto Longhi) of influential journal *Paragone*; best known for *Artemisia* (1947), an imagined biography of artist Artemisia Gentileschi.

Baricco, Alessandro (1958-). Contemporary novelist, interested in theatre, music and innovative forms of television; successful novels combine lyrical style, fantasy elements and mystery (e.g. *Oceano mare*, 1993; *Seta*, 1996).

Bassani, Giorgio (1916-2000). Important novelist, as well as poet and cultural operator; chronicler of mid-century Ferrara in novel-cycle *Il romanzo di Ferrara* (1956-74); best-known work *Il giardino dei Finzi-Contini* (1962), set in the Jewish community of Ferrara under Fascism; discovered Tomasi di Lampedusa's *Il gattopardo* when editor at Feltrinelli.

Bazlen, Roberto (Bobi) (1902-65). Influential intellectual figure for mid-century; close to Montale, and to German-language culture; worked for Einaudi and Bompiani before setting up Adelphi publishers.

Bellezza, Dario (1944-96). Gay poet and novelist, influenced by Pasolini among others (see *Morte di Pasolini*, 1981); often focused in his work on intense, self-destructive pleasures of gay sex and drugs and anti-conformist polemic; died of AIDS.

Bene, Carmelo (1937-2002). Dominant figure in avant-garde theatre in Italy from 1960s onwards, with expressionistic, physical performance style; known especially for radical reworkings of classics such as *Pinocchio* and *Amleto* (both 1962).

Benni, Stefano (1947-). Comic novelist, moving between science-fiction (*Terra!*, 1981) and satire (*Bar sport*, 1976); player of rich linguistic games; also works in journalism

Bertolucci, Attilio (1911-2000). Important lyric poet, associated with landscape, natural cycles and autobiographical narratives from his native Romagna region; long career from first collection *Sirio* (1929) to long verse-narrative *La camera da letto* (1984-88); father of filmmaker Bernardo.

Betti, Ugo (1892-1953). Playwright and judge (until purged from his job after fall of Fascism); prisoner of war with Gadda in First World War; works include *Frana allo scalo nord* (1935), about justice and corruption.

Bilenchi, Romano (1909-89). Tuscan novelist; in young Fascist and Florentine literary circles in 1920s and 1930s, but moved to become a Communist and fought in the Resistance.

Bobbio, Norberto (1909-2004). Influential liberal philosopher and public intellectual; part of key generation of Turinese anti-Fascist intellectuals; specialist in jurisprudence, but generally influential in steering a middle course between left and right in political philosophy.

Bontempelli, Massimo (1878-1960). Author of fantastic, modernist novels and plays (e.g. *Nostra dea*, 1925); co-founder with Malaparte of innovative, cosmopolitan journal *900* (1926-29) where he developed notion of 'realismo magico'; associated with Fascism.

Borgese, Giuseppe Antonio (1882-1952). Novelist, critic, moralist and anti-Fascist exile; author of important anti-heroic novel *Rubé* (1921).

Brancati, Vitaliano (1907-54). Novelist and playwright characterised by satirical take on his native Sicilian society; moved away from early Fascism; major works include *Don Giovanni in Sicilia* (1941) and *Il bell'Antonio* (1949); had trouble with censors both during and after Fascism, for the sexual and moral aspects of his work.

Bruck, Edith (1932-). Novelist and Holocaust survivor; born in Hungary, settled in Italy in 1950s; works include Holocaust memoir *Chi ti ama così* (1958).

Bufalino, Gesualdo (1920-96). Sicialian novelist who came to prominence late, at the age of 61, with *Diceria dell'untore* (1981), set in a TB sanatorium in the1940s; notable for his highly literary, baroque style.

Busi, Aldo (1948-). Prolific, flamboyantly gay novelist; linguistically rich and sexually explicit; works include *Seminario della gioventù* (1984) and *Vita standard di un venditore provvisorio di collant* (1985).

Buzzati, Dino (1906-72). Novelist, short-story writer, playwright and longtime journalist for *Corriere della sera*; work characterised by a darkly allegorical, fantastic aura, often compared to Kafka or absurdist literature; best-known novel *Il deserto dei Tartari* (1940).

Calasso, Roberto (1941-). Director of Adelphi publishing house, responsible for important translations of Nietzsche and a wide range of Central European writers; author of grand retellings of myth cycles, from European (*Le nozze di Cadmo e Armonia*, 1988) to Buddhist (*Ka*, 1996).

Calvino, Italo (1923-85). Perhaps the dominant figure in postwar Italian literature; began writing Resistance narrative close to Neo-Realism (e.g. *Il sentiero dei nidi di ragno*, 1947); while maintaining a realist vein of work, moved into modern fable with the trilogy *I nostri antenati* (1951-9); followed by a long experimental phase (influenced by contacts with European figures such as structuralism and the OULIPO group in Paris), from science-fantasy stories (e.g. *Cosmicomiche*, 1965) to lyrical fantasies of imaginary spaces (*Le città invisibili*, 1972) to postmodern games with reading and literature (*Se una notte d'inverno un viaggiatore,* 1979); also a highly influential essayist and editorial consultant for the Einaudi publishing house.

Camilleri, Andrea (1925-). Worked in theatre and television before achieving huge success from 1994 with a series of detective stories about the Sicilian Inspector Montalbano, using a mix of standard Italian and Sicilian.

Camon, Ferdinando (1935-). Poet, novelist, critic; interested in giving voice to marginalised groups and classes, especially related to his native province near Padua.

Campana, Dino (1885-1932). Visionary poet; between periods of travel and confinement in asylums for mental illness, wrote *Canti orfici* (1914), a rich cycle of hallucinatory verse and prose poems; influenced by French symbolists.

Capriolo, Paola (1962-). Contemporary novelist with a lucid philosophical edge and an interest in fantasy; works include *La grande Eulalia* (1988), *Un uomo di carattere* (1996).

Caproni, Giorgio (1912-90). Poet; early work influenced by Saba, among others; wrote with modest voice and strong rhythms about difficult themes; works include *Congedo del viaggiatore cerimonioso* (1965).

Cardarelli, Vincenzo (1887-1959). Influential prose and poetry writer of early decades of century; part of group around *La Voce* in early twentieth-century Florence, until returning to classical models through his journal *La Ronda* (1919-23) and his elegant, highly crafted style of 'prosa d'arte'; supporter of Fascism in 1920s and 1930s.

Cassola, Carlo (1917-87). Novelist, associated with Neo-Realism; wrote about working people, the war, the Resistance and its aftermath, the emotions of everyday life; major works include *Fausto e Anna* (1952), *La ragazza di Bube* (1960).

Cecchi, Emilio (1884-1966). Conservative essayist, writer of 'prosa d'arte', influential literature and art critic and journalist; involved in key journals in early twentieth-century Florence (*Leonardo, La Voce, La Ronda*); later a travel writer (*America amara*, 1939) and worked in cinema.

Celati, Gianni (1937-). Novelist, interested in oral culture and in American popular culture; significant works have explored youthful rebellion (e.g. *Lunario del paradiso*, 1978) and local voices of the Po valley (*Narratori delle pianure*, 1984); important link from postwar generation to young generations of writers in 1970s and 1980s.

Cialente, Fausta (1898-1993). Novelist, anti-Fascist, based for some time in Egypt.

Comisso, Giovanni (1895-1916). Author of stories, novels and travel literature; isolated from mainstream, partly because of homosexuality and interest in peasant and non-Eurpoean cultures.

Consolo, Vincenzo (1933-). Novelist; key figure in contemporary Sicilian writing, alongside Gesualdo Bufalino; uses complex narrative techniques and style; interested in memory, history and language; best known for *Il sorriso dell'ignoto marinaio* (1976).

Contini, Gianfranco (1912-90). Brilliant textual and literary critic; impact on twentieth-century literature came in particular through his work on Dante's 'plurilingualism' and his seminal essays on Gadda, Montale, Pasolini and other contemporaries, which helped established their reputations.

Corazzini, Sergio (1886-1907). Poet associated with 'crepuscolari' movement; work tinged with melancholy and death; died young of TB.

Croce, Benedetto (1866-1952). Idealist philosopher, critic and historian; dominant figure in Italian intellectual culture for much of the century; renowned for his dignified anti-Fascism (drafted the 'Manifesto degli intellettuali antifascisti', 1925); influential aesthetic of literature as located in essential, intuitive moments of 'poesia'.

D'Annunzio, Gabriele (1863-1938). Poet, novelist, playwright and iconic figure of late nineteenth-century Italian literature; major works mostly before 1900 but continued writing and remained a looming presence in early twentieth century; campaigned for intervention in First World War, undertook military adventures (e.g. occupation of Fiume, 1919-21) and was model for Mussolini.

D'Arrigo, Stefano (1919-92). Novelist best known for one massive, sprawling, stylistically complex work set in wartime Naples and Sicily, *Horcynus Orca* (1975).

Debenedetti, Giacomo (1901-67). Critic interested in psychoanlysis; also author of significant, short narrative works about Italian Jews under Fascism and Nazi occupation (e.g. *16 ottobre 1943*, 1944).

De Carlo, Andrea (1952-). Contemporary novelist, interested in post-1968 generation; works include *Treno di panna* (1981), set in Los Angeles, and *Due di due* (1989).

De Cespedes, Alba (1911-97). Novelist and editor of important literary journal *Mercurio* (1944-48); feminist novels focus on women's experience, from debut *Nessuno torna indietro* (1938), which was censored by Fascists, to postwar works such as *Quaderno proibito* (1952).

De Filippo, Eduardo (1900-84). Charismatic Neapolitan playwright, actor-director and company leader (with his brother and sister); author of large body of plays in Italian and Neapolitan dialect; influenced by popular theatre traditions as well as by Pirdandello; major works include *Napoli milionaria!* (1945), *Filumena Marturano* (1946), *Sabato, Domenica, Lunedì* (1959).

Deledda, Grazia (1871-36). Sardinian novelist in 'verista' (realist) tradition; mature works include *Elias Portolu* (1904) and *Canne al vento* (1913); awarded Nobel Prize for Literature, 1920.

Delfini, Antonio (1907-1963). Writer influenced by surrealism and fantastic literature, whose work was rediscovered in the 1980s; works include *Fanalino della Battimonda* (1930), *Diari* (1982).

Del Giudice, Daniele (1949-). Sophisticated contemporary novelist, interested in science, perception and alienation; works include *Lo stadio di Wimbledon* (1983), *Atlante occidentale* (1985), *Staccando l'ombra da terra* (1994).

Duranti, Francesca (1935-). Novelist, interested in interplay of reality and fiction; came to prominence with *La casa sul lago della luna* (1984).

Eco, Umberto (1932-). Semiotician and novelist; close to 'neo-avaguardia' in the 1960s; wrote influential works on mass culture (*Apocalittici e integrati*, 1964) and textual interpretation (*Opera aperta*, 1962); has continued to write semiotic theory, regular journalism and, later, philosophy; from 1980 launched a hugely successful further career as a 'postmodern' novelist (*Il nome della rosa*, 1980; *Il pendolo di Foucault*, 1988); internationally known cultural figure.

Fabbri, Diego (1911-80). Playwright, with religious concerns; favoured using legal framework for his drama; most significant work *Processo a Gesù* (1955).

Fallaci, Oriana (1929-). Politically committed, feminist journalist and writer; interviewed key historical figures in *Intervista con la storia* (1974); tackled abortion in *Lettera a un bambino mai nato* (1975); and controversially raged against the attacks of 11 September 2001 in *La rabbia e l'orgoglio* (2001).

Fenoglio, Beppe (1922-63). Novelist and central figure in literature of the Resistance; major work *Il partigiano Johnny* (1968), published after his death, collated from incomplete manuscripts; experimented with use of an idiosyncratic English in his work.

Ferrante, Elena (d.o.b. unknown). Reclusive contemporary novelist, associated with Naples; author of intense narratives about contemporary women's lives, *L'amore molesto* (1992), *I giorni dell'abbandono* (2002).

Flaiano, Ennio (1910-72). Journalist, writer and screenwriter; wrote for Fellini, Antonioni and others; key part of Roman scene of 1950s; author of *Tempo di uccidere* (1947), about the war in Abyssinia.

Fo, Dario (1926-). Comic performer and playwright; author of large number of plays and sketches, mostly farces with a radical left-wing political edge, often written or refined in collaboration with his wife Franca Rame; influenced by medieval popular 'giullare' tradition; major works include *Morte accidentale dell'anarchico* (1970), *Mistero buffo* (first performed 1969); winner of Nobel Prize for Literature, 1997.

Fortini, Franco (1917-95) (pseud. Franco Lattes). Poet, critic, translator and essayist; after the Resistance, worked on Vittorini's *Il Politecnico*, then for Olivetti, publishers, schools and universities; key dissident intellectual on the left, critical of PCI and of mass culture (e.g. essays in *Verifica dei poteri*, 1965); wrote several volumes of poetry.

Fruttero, Carlo (1926-) and **Franco Lucentini** (1920-2002). Together contributed to flourishing of several popular genres: science-fiction and comics through their editing of series and magazines; and, especially, detective fiction through their own works, from *La donna della domenica* (1972) onwards.

Gadda, Carlo Emilio (1983-1973). Writer and engineer; one of the greatest and most linguistically and philosophically difficult writers of the century; much of his work in fragments; soldier and prisoner-of-war in First World War, sympathetic to Fascism; only became widely known with (re)publication of two major novels, *Quer pasticciaccio brutto de via Merulana* (1957) and *La cognizione del dolore* (1963).

Gatto, Alfonso (1909-76). Poet; close to hermeticism, but also politically committed following Resistance experience and attached to landscape of Southern Italy.

Gentile, Giovanni (1875-1944). Philosopher, initially close to and influenced by Croce, but the two diverged and Gentile became a prominent Fascist thinker and minister; responsible for education reform in 1920s and for the *Enciclopedia italiana* project in 1930s.

Ginzburg, Carlo (1939-). Innovative historian and son of Natalia and

Leone Ginzburg; work combines microhistorical research (on witch trials, heresies etc) and narrative interpretation; e.g. *Il formaggio e i vermi* (1976).

Ginzburg, Natalia (1916-91). Novelist; formed in Turinese, Jewish, anti-Fascist intellectual family (described in memoir *Lessico famigliare*, 1963); worked for Einaudi; narrative works characterised by studiedly spare, dialogue-driven language, everyday, often family-related experience and characters who have limited insight into their lives; major works include *Tutti i nostri ieri* (1952), *Le voci della sera* (1961), *Caro Michele* (1973).

Giudici, Giovanni (1924-). Poet, characterised by autobiographical, non-lyric idiom; influenced by Montale and 'crepuscolari'; translated Russian and English poetry; worked for Olivetti.

Gozzano, Guido (1883-1916). Most important poet of 'crepuscolare' grouping; key works *La via del rifugio* (1907) and *I colloqui* (1911) characterised by an ironic, witty voice, acutely aware of its own inadequacies, provincial (Piedmontese) settings, and a subtle use of rhythm and verse-form; died young of TB.

Gramsci, Antonio (1891-1937). Major Marxist thinker; began as socialist activist in Turin and was one of the founders of the breakaway PCI in 1921; arrested and imprisoned in 1926 until shortly before his premature death; in prison wrote the highly influential *Quaderni del carcere* (published from 1947), notebooks on issues in Marxist theory, Italian culture, politics and history.

Guareschi, Giovanno (1908-68). Novelist, best known for 'Don Camillo' series of comic novels, begun in 1948, centred on the bickering pair of a priest and a Communist mayor in a small town; also a nationalist and anti-Communist satirical journalist.

Guerra, Tonino (1920-). Dialect poet from Romagna (e.g. *I scarabócc*, 1946), novelist and screenwriter for Antonioni, Fellini and others.

Jahier, Piero (1884-1966). Poet and novelist; part of *La Voce* grouping; marked by Waldensian religious upbringing; anti-Fascist; works include autobiographical *Con me e con gli alpini* (1920).

Jovine, Francesco (1902-50). Neo-Realist writer; fought in Resistance; work set in Molise region, including his best-known novel *Le terre del sacramento* (1950), about the peasants struggle for land in the early 1920s.

La Capria, Raffaele (1922-). Neapolitan novelist and critic.

Lampedusa, see **Tomasi di Lampedusa**

Landolfi, Tommaso (1908-79). Novelist and story-writer associated with fantastic or surreal invention and a refined style; close to hermeticism, influenced by Leopardi, Poe and Gogol. among others; narrative concerns include gambling, loss, violence, metamorphosis.

Ledda, Gavino (1938-). Sardinian writer, best known for his autobiographical first work, *Padre padrone* (1975) about his escape from his rural childhood and authoritarian father.

Leonetti, Francesco (1924-). Politically committed poet, novelist and intellectual associated with several key postwar journals and movements (*Officina*, 1955-9, *Il menabò*, 1959-67, 'neo-avanguardia', *Alfabeta*, 1979-88).

Levi, Carlo (1902-75). Turinese doctor, painter, writer; joined 'Giustizia e libertà' anti-Fascist group, was arrested and sent to internal exile in Basilicata, recalled in his most famous work *Cristo si è fermato a Eboli* (1945); after this, became campaigner for Southern Italy (*Le parole sono pietre*, 1955).

Levi, Primo (1919-87). Widely admired writer and Holocaust survivor (*Se questo è un uomo*, 1947; *I sommersi e i salvati*, 1987); bridged literature-science divide in his work on his career in industrial chemistry (*Il sistema periodico*, 1975) and in his science-fiction (*Storie naturali*, 1966; *Vizio di forma*, 1971); eclectic essayist (*L'altrui mestiere*, 1985); committed suicide.

Loi, Franco (1930-). Dialect poet in Milanese; most ambitious work is long, autobiographical sequence, *L'angel* (1981).

Loy, Rosetta (1931-). Accomplished contemporary novelist whose works include the historical family saga *La strada di polvere* (1987) and a memoir and historical enquiry into treatment of Jews in Fascist Rome, *La parola ebreo* (1997).

Lucarelli, Carlo (1960-). One of the most interesting figures in contemporary wave of crime writers, in fiction (e.g. *Almost Blue*, 1997) and on television.

Lucentini, Franco, see under **Fruttero, Carlo**

Lussu, Emilio (1890-1975). Sardinian anti-Fascist politician and writer; founder member of 'Giustizia e libertà' in exile in Paris; author of memoir narratives on rise of Fascism (*La marcia su Roma e dintorni*, 1933) and on First World War (*Un anno sull'altipiano*, 1938).

Luzi, Mario (1914-). One of the major poets of the century, associated with Florentine hermeticism; influences include French symbolism and Catholic modernism, as well as Eliot and Montale; collections range over seventy years, including *La barca* (1935), *Primizie del deserto* (1953), *Viaggio terrestre e celeste di Simone Martini* (1994).

Magrelli, Valerio (1957-). Poet, characterised by lucid, philosophical lyrics and perceptions of contemporary life (e.g. *Ora serrata retinae*, 1980; *Nature e venature*, 1987).

Magris, Claudio (1939-). Triestine critic and writer; authority on Central European culture; best-known for *Danubio* (1986), a sophisticated literary travelogue.

Malaparte, Curzio (1898-1957) (pseud. Kurt Erich Suckert). Controversial Tuscan writer and journalist; fought in First World War, prominent Fascist before falling out with the regime; leading figure in 'strapaese' movement; author of brilliant polemics; roaming war journalism in Second World War led to two rich novels *Kaputt* (1944) and *La pelle* (1949).

Malerba, Luigi (1927-) (pseud. Luigi Bonardi). Novelist, member of 'neo-avanguardia'; writing characterised by surreal and comic or grotesque elements; works include *La scoperta dell'alfabeto* (1963), *Il pianeta azzurro* (1986).

Manganelli, Giorgio (1932-90). Sophisticated novelist and essayist (e.g. *Letteratura come menzogna*, 1967); member of 'neo-avanguardia'; work characterised by scepticism, formal experimentation and linguistic richness (comparable to Gadda); also art critic, travel writer, translator.

Manzini, Gianna (1896-1974). Novelist; part of group of intellectuals around *Solaria* and other Florentine journals; influenced by Virginia Woolf, her work is characterised by blurring between fiction, history and autobiography and by temporal fragmentation (e.g. *Lettera all'editore*, 1945).

Maraini, Dacia (1936-). Contemporary feminist writer; wide range of work in fiction, autobiography, journalism; novels include *L'età del malessere* (1963), *Memorie di una ladra* (1972), *La lunga vita di Marianna Ucrìa* (1990); she has also worked extensively in theatre, including a women's company 'la Maddalena'.

Marin, Biagio (1891-1985). Dialect poet from Grado (near Trieste); early contact with *La Voce* group; focus on local life and its fragilities, expressed in pure, melodic style; poems collected in *I canti dell'isola* (1985).

Marinetti, Filippo Tommaso (1876-1944). Poet, playwright, novelist, cultural operator; formed in Egypt and in symbolist literary circles in Paris, then founder and animator of the Futurist movement, from 1909 to his death; author of many manifestoes, collage poems, plays and several Futurist novels (e.g. *Mafarka le futuriste*, 1909); interventionist and close to Mussolini and Fascism.

Masino, Paola (1908-89). Novelist, poet, journalist; companion of Bontempelli; works include experimental satirical novel *Nascita e morte della massaia* (1939).

Mastronardi, Lucio (1930-79). Novelist and teacher; author of comic novels about his Lombardy hometown, Vigevano (e.g. *Il maestro di Vigevano*, 1962).

Meneghello, Luigi (1922-). Writer from Veneto, who fought in the Resistance and then taught in England (Reading University) from 1940s on; novels mostly autobiographical, interested in language, with ironic perspectives on, e.g., his hometown Malo (*Libera nos a Malo*, 1963), the Resistance (*I piccoli maestri*, 1964), exile (*Il dispatrio*, 1993).

Michelstaedter, Carlo (1882-1910). Precocious thinker and writer from Gorizia, of Jewish origin, who committed suicide aged 28; had contact with *La Voce* group in Florence; his eccentric, pessimistic treatise *La persuasione e la rettorica* appeared in 1913.

Montale, Eugenio (1896-1981). The most important Italian poet of the century; reputation built on first three collections, *Ossi di seppia* (1924), *Le occasioni* (1939) and *La bufera e altro* (1956), characterised by Ligurian landscapes, meditations on metaphysical malaise, enigmatic interactions with a shifting female 'tu', tellingly symbolic objects; later collections (from *Satura*, 1975, onwards) more ironic and prosaic in style; also active cultural operator and journalist; awarded Nobel Prize for Literature, 1975.

Morante, Elsa (1912-85). Author of four long, dense and highly sophisticated novels: *Menzogna e sortilegio* (1948), *L'isola di Arturo* (1957), *La storia* (1974) and *Aracoeli* (1982); recurrent concerns include childhood, sexual identity and dependence, mothers and sons/daughters, the fictions of writing and memory, obsession, abjection; also wrote some poetry, children's stories, essays.

Moravia, Alberto (1907-90) (pseud. Alberto Pincherle). Long considered a major novelist of the century, his reputation has faded somewhat in recent years; his early debut *Gli indifferenti* (1929) stood out for its direct prose and its critique of bourgeois mores (taken by some as anti-Fascist); later novels were interested in the psychology of alienation and boredom, often seen through a sexual perspective (*La noia*, 1960), and in the working classes (*La romana*, 1947; *Racconti romani*, 1954); an active cultural operator in Rome, he co-founded the review *Nuovi argomenti* (1953-), wrote essays, reviews and travel writing; he had long-term relationships with Elsa Morante and Dacia Maraini.

Morselli, Guido (1912-73). Novelist, only discovered after his death by suicide; author of realist novels, satires and historical inventions.

Negri, Ada (1870-1945). Poet, novelist, teacher of working-class origin; supported the Fascist regime.

Noventa, Giacomo (1898-1960). Poet who wrote in a hybrid Veneto dialect of his own invention, with a varied and forceful voice distinct from mainstream; anti-Fascist who knew Gobetti in Turin and *Solaria* group in Florence.

Ortese, Anna Maria (1914-98). Novelist and journalist; went through loosely Neo-Realist phase (e.g. *Il mare non bagna Napoli*, 1953), but mature work characterised by a fantastic, visionary style, in novels such as *L'iguana* (1965) *Il porto di Toledo* (1975), *Il cardillo addolorato* (1993).

Ottieri, Ottiero (1924-2002). Novelist; worked for Olivetti and best-known as a contributor of essays and novels to the 'Literature and industry' debates of the 1960s.

Pagliarani, Elio (1927-). Experimental poet, included in the anthology *I novissimi* (1961) which helped launch the 'neo-avanguardia'.

Palazzeschi, Aldo (1885-1974) (pseud. Aldo Giurlani). Eccentric and playful poet and novelist, close first to 'crepuscolari' and then Futurists, under whose auspices he wrote a manifesto ('Il controdolore', 1914), poetry (*L'incendiario*, 1910) and narrative (*Il codice di Perelà*, 1911); successful later work included the novel *Le sorelle Materassi*, (1934).

Papini, Giovanni (1881-1956). Writer and one of the key movers in Florentine culture of the early twentieth century; heavily involved with journals *Leonardo*, *La Voce*, *Lacerba* and briefly allied to Futurism; in dialogue with Croce and many others; author of autobiographical novel, *Un uomo finito* (1912); later turned to Catholicism and supported Fascist regime.

Parise, Goffredo (1929-86). Novelist and travel writer with markedly original voice; works included elements of fantasy, satire (*Il padrone*,

1965) and the alphabetically arranged vignettes of *Sillabario* (two vols, 1972 and 1982).

Pascoli, Giovanni (1855-1912). Important poet of the late nineteenth century, whose socialism, lyric and linguistic freshness, and musicality made him an important influence on twentieth-century poetry and literary language (e.g. on 'crepuscolari', dialect poets, Saba, Pasolini, Betolucci); later work more nationalist in flavour.

Pasolini, Pier Paolo (1922-75). Poet (e.g. *Le ceneri di Gramsci*, 1958), novelist (e.g. *Ragazzi di vita*, 1955), journalist (e.g. *Lettere luterane*, 1975), critic and filmmaker; highly creative and controversial figure in both cultural and political terms, in part owing to his homosexuality; animator of important journal, *Officina* (1955-9), which merged 'impegno' with stylistic analysis; worked in Friulan and Roman dialects as well as standard Italian, before moving into film in 1960s, although continued to write poetry, plays, novel fragments (e.g. *Petrolio*, 1992); apocalyptic critic of modern consumer society; murdered in 1975.

Pavese, Cesare (1908-50). Turinese novelist and poet; work characterised by Piedmontese landscape, an elaborate mythology of nature, a contrast of city to country, and weak (mostly male) protagonists; often seen as part of Neo-Realism; key works include the novels *La casa in collina* (1948) and *La luna e i falò* (1950), the diary *Il mestiere di vivere* (1952), and the poetry of *Lavorare stanca* (1936); anti-Fascist, influential translator of American literature, editor at Einaudi; committed suicide.

Penna, Sandro (1906-77). Poet; wrote in direct, clear and simple language, typically in quatrains, most often evoking his homosexual experiences; both theme and style set him apart from dominant trends in modern poetry.

Piovene, Guido (1907-74). Aristocratic Catholic novelist, travel writer and journalist; wrote honestly about collusion with Fascism.

Pirandello, Luigi (1867-1936). Prolific Sicilian writer of novels (e.g. *Il fu Mattia Pascal*, 1904; *Uno nessuno e centomila*, 1926), short stories (collected as *Novelle per un anno*) and, most importantly, plays; obsessive concern with the complications, paradoxes and ironies of identity; his experimental plays (e.g. *Sei personaggi in cerca d'autore*, 1921; *Enrico IV*, 1922) were hugely influential for modern European theatre and for modernism generally; also wrote for and about cinema; supporter of Fascism.

Pitigrilli (1893-1975) (pseud. Dino Segre). Turinese popular author of erotic and social genre novels between the wars; converted from Judaism to Catholicism; spied for Fascist secret police.

Porta, Antonio (1935-89). Poet from Milan, included in the anthology *I novissimi* (1961) which helped launch the 'neo-avanguardia'.

Pratolini, Vasco (1913-91). Novelist associated with Neo-Realism and with chronicles of the Florentine working classes in series of novels of 1940s (e.g. *Il quartiere*, 1944; *Cronache di poveri amanti*, 1947); caused controversy on the Neo-Realist left with the historical novel *Metello* (1955) and the epic portrayal of Fascist Florence in *Lo scialo* (1960).

Pressburger, Giorgio (1937-). Novelist; born in Hungary, emigrated to Italy with twin brother Nicola after 1956; first wrote stories about Budapest (with his brother), then novels drawing on his medical training.

Prezzolini, Giuseppe (1882-1992). Key figure in early twentieth-century Florence, together with Papini; founded *Leonardo* and *La Voce* and was a strong voice for cultural renewal; subsequently moved to America and wrote essays and memoirs.

Quasimodo, Salvatore (1901-68). Major poet, associated with the hermetic generation of Ungaretti and Montale; his early work is steeped in the enchanted landscape of Sicily, with a undertow of loss and melancholy (*Ed è subito sera*, 1942); later poetry more open to contemporary reality; awarded Nobel Prize for Literature, 1959.

Raboni, Giovanni (1932-). Milanese poet and critic; also active journalist and translator. Verse is formally aware and combines somewhat detached personal voice with urban, public dimension; collected in *A tanto caro sangue* (1988).

Rame, Franca (1929-). Feminist actress, playwright, wife of Dario Fo and co-responsible for almost his entire output; her own monologues on women's experiences, including rape (based on her own kidnap and rape) an important product of 1970s feminism.

Ramondino, Fabrizia (1936-). Neapolitan novelist, best known for *Althénopis*, a mother-daughter narrative set in wartime Naples.

Rea, Domenico (1921-94). Neapolitan novelist, best known for stories in *Spaccanapoli* (1947), a key Neo-Realist work.

Rebora, Clemente (1885-1957). Milanese poet with early associations with *La Voce* (*Frammenti lirici*, 1913); converted to Catholicism and religious verse in 1929 (and later ordained).

Revelli, Nuto (1919-). Writer and oral historian, of the Russian campaign and the Resistance in Second World War (e.g. *Mai tardi*, 1946) and of Piedmont peasantry (*Il mondo dei vinti*, 1977); close to other memorialists, Rigoni Stern and Primo Levi.

Rigoni Stern, Mario (1921-). Writer, best known for *Il sergente della neve* (1953), about the awful Russian front in Second World War; close to other memorialists, Revelli and Primo Levi.

Romano, Lalla (1906-2001). Poet and later novelist; series of autobiographical novels, about the war, family; including *Le parole tra noi leggere* (1969), about a mother-son relationship.

Rosselli, Amelia (1930-96). Multilingual (Italian, English, French) poet; daughter of assassinated anti-Fascist Carlo Rosselli; wrote highly sophisticated, formally experimental poetry with intense motifs of desire and death (e.g. *Variazioni belliche*, 1964; *La libellula* 1985); subject to depression, she committed suicide.

Rosso di San Secondo, Pier Maria (1887-1956). Sicilian playwright (e.g. *Marionette che passione!*, 1918), associated with Pirandellian themes and with the so-called 'teatro del grottesco', alongside Luigi Chiarelli, Enrico Cavacchioli and Luigi Antonelli.

Roversi, Roberto (1923-). Poet, co-founder of *Officina* (1955-9), with Pasolini and Leonetti.

Saba, Umberto (1883-57). Triestine poet of Jewish origin; poetry characterised by autobiographical elements and the everyday life of Trieste, evoked in direct and simple language with regular metre and form; collected in *Canzoniere* (1st edition 1919, then gradually enlarged throughout his life, including his own commentary after 1947); also wrote prose fragments (*Scorciatoie*, 1946) and a posthumously published novel, *Ernesto* (1975), about a boy's homosexual experience.

Sanguineti, Edoardo (1930-). Poet, novelist, theorist and academic; central figure in 'neo-avanguardia'; experimental poetry mixes languages, irregular forms, dense labyrinthine patterns of meaning (e.g. *Laborintus*, 1956); novels mixed experimentalism and influence of French 'nouveau roman' (e.g. *Capriccio italiano*, 1961); has also written drama and opera librettos and edited an influential anthology of modern verse.

Sanvitale, Francesca (1928-). Accomplished contemporary novelist, whose best-known work is *Madre e figlia* (1980).

Savinio, Alberto (1891-1952) (pseud. Andrea De Chirico). Writer, composer, painter, brother of artist Giorgio De Chirico; in contact with Parisian circles (Apollinaire, Picasso, surrealists, Cocteau, etc.), wrote the important experimental novel *Hermaphrodito* (1918).

Sbarbaro, Camillo (1888-1967). Ligurian poet, first published by *La Voce*; subdued emphasis on objects; early influence on Montale.

Scerbanenco, Giorgio (1911-69). Genre novelist born in Kiev; wrote romantic stories, and from 1966, detective novels (e.g. *Venere privata*, 1966).

Sciascia, Leonardo (1921-89). Most important Sicilian writer of postwar period; began as teacher in his native Racalmuto (see *Le parocchie di Regalpetra*, 1956) and developed pessimistic vision of Sicilian history and present, rooted in Enlightenment values, in detective novels about the mafia (e.g. *Il giorno della civetta*, 1961; *A ciascuno il suo*, 1966) and in historical fictions or archive investigations (e.g. *Il consiglio d'Egitto*, 1973; *Morte dell'Inquisitore*, 1964); wrote a powerful response to murder of Aldo Moro, *L'affaire Moro* (1978).

Scotellaro, Rocco (1923-53). Writer, poet and socialist campaigner for Southern poor; poetry and unfinished novel *L'uva puttanella* (1956) published posthumously.

Sereni, Vittorio (1913-83). Important poet for the generation moving away from hermeticism and towards a more everyday idiom, with subtle metrics and lyric qualities beneath the surface; prisoner-of-war in Algeria in 1940s, evoked in *Diario d'Algeria* (1947).

Silone, Ignazio (1900-78) (pseud. Secondo Tranquilli). Political activist, writer and moralist, from Abruzzo region; one of founders of PCI in 1921, an anti-Fascist activist, then exile in Switzerland in 1920s; fell out with the party having seen Stalin at work (*Uscita di sicurezza*, 1965) and turned to literature; first novel *Fontamara* (1933, in German translation) became international success for its fable-like denunciation of Fascism; further novels and essays in exile followed (*Pane e vino*, 1936; *La scuola dei dittatori*, 1938); back in postwar Italy, later work became increasingly Christian in outlook; involved with *Tempo presente* (later revealed as CIA-funded) and recently accused of informing to Fascist police during 1920s.

Sinisgalli, Leonardo (1908-81). Poet and engineer who brought science and mathematics into his lyrics (e.g. *Quaderno di geometria*, 1936) and prose pieces; close to hermetics.

Slataper, Scipio (1888-1915). One of a group of Triestine writers drawn to Florentine circles around *La Voce*; interventionist, then nationalist; best known for the autobiographical text *Il mio Carso* (1912).

Soffici, Ardengo (1879-1964). Poet, painter and critic; brought Parisian influences back to Florence; part of Florentine group around *La Voce*, *Lacerba*; author of autobiographical novel *Lemmonio Boreo* (1911); later a convinced Fascist and supporter of 'strapaese' movement.

Soldati, Mario (1906-99). Writer, screenwriter and film-director; spent time in America (*America primo amore*, 1935); author of large number of vivid, well-written novels.

Solmi, Serigo (1899-1981). Poet, critic; fought in both First World War and Resistance; poetry open to prosaic discourse; translator.

Stuparich, Giani (1891-1961). One of several Triestine writers drawn to Florentine circles around *La Voce*, including his brother Carlo; wrote a diary and novel about First World War; anti-Fascist; author of autobiographical and fictional prose.

Svevo, Italo (1861-1928) (pseud. Ettore Schmitz). One of the major figures in Italian and European modernism; born and lived in Trieste, of Jewish origin; worked in a bank and a shipping-paint firm; influenced by Darwin, Schopenhauer and Freud; close to James Joyce, who taught him English in Trieste after 1907 (and a model for Joyce's Leopold Bloom); author of three major novels, *Una vita* (1892), *Senilità* (1898) and, after a long gap, the extraordinary *La coscienza di Zeno* (1923), a mixed-up, comic self-analysis of indecision and philandering by the infuriating anti-hero, Zeno Cosini; also wrote a number of plays and essays.

Tabucchi, Antonio (1943-). Contemporary novelist and academic; influenced especially by Portuguese writer Fernando Pessoa and 'magic realist' tradition; best known for enigmatic stories and novels, with mysterious ambiences and elusive meanings, often with political undertow; including *Il gioco del rovescio* (1981), *Piccoli equivoci senza importanza* (1985), and the detective novel set in Portugal, *Sostiene Pereira* (1994).

Tamaro, Susanna (1957-). Novelist; achieved huge success with sentimental simplicity of *Va' dove ti porta il cuore* (1997).

Tessa, Delio (1886-1939). Milanese dialect poet; anti-Fascist; best known work, *L'è el dì di mort, alegher!* (1932).

Testori, Giovanni (1923-93). Milanese novelist, poet and playwright, with strong unorthodox religious dimension; author of violently vivid works about the underclasses of Milan (e.g. *L'Arialda*, 1961) and of experimental plays (e.g. *L'Ambleto*, 1972); religious.

Tomasi di Lampedusa, Giuseppe (1896-1957). Aristocratic Sicilian whose masterpiece was a historical novel about the Sicilian 'Risorgimento', *Il gattopardo* (published posthumously in 1958, thanks to Giorgio Bassani and Feltrinelli publishers).

Tomizza, Fulvio (1935-). Novelist associated with Istria, near Yugoslav border, split between Italian and Slav identity.

Tondelli, Pier Vittorio (1955-91). Pivotal writer of generation emerging at the end of 1970s; key gay writer of the period and chronicler of cosmopolitan youth culture, in often explicit stories and novels (*Altri libertini*, 1980) and journalism (*Un weekend postmoderno*, 1990); last novel *Camere separate* (1989) more conventional, about a gay relationship overshadowed by AIDS, of which Tondelli was to die; influential sponsor of other, young writers (e.g. with *Under 25* project).

Tozzi, Federigo (1883-1920). Sienese novelist; author of dark narratives of psychological weakness and destruction, with Tuscan settings and autobiographical elements (e.g. *Con gli occhi chiusi*, 1919; *Tre croci*, 1920).

Trilussa (1871-1950) (pseud. Carlo Alberto Salustri). Popular Roman dialect poet, author of comic, fable-like and satirical sketches of Roman life.

Ungaretti, Giuseppe (1888-1970). One of the most important poets of the century; raised in Alexandria, Egypt, then moved to Paris and avant-garde art circles; fought in First World War, leading to sequence of spare, fragmentary, powerful poems about exile and war, the core of his first major collection *L'allegria* (1931); second collection *Sentimento del tempo* (1933) saw a return to fuller verse-forms and to the classical and literary tradition; in Brazil, 1936-42; later poetry more religious, including the anguished *Il dolore* (1947) about the death of his son; close to Mussolini and Fascism, but also cosmopolitan; poetry collected as *Vita d'un uomo*.

Valduga, Patrizia (1952-). Contemporary poet; combines intense themes of suffering and sexuality with classical Petrarchan forms; first collection *Medicamenta* (1982).

Vassalli, Sebastiano (1941-). One of the most interesting novelists of the last two decades of the century; after experimental early works, author of varied novels touching on Italy's history, cultural and national identity, including the historical novel *La chimera* (1990), science-fiction (*3012*, 1995) and a fictionalised biography of the poet Dino Campana (*La notte della cometa*, 1985).

Viganò, Renata (1900-76). Novelist, best known for Neo-Realist Resistance novel, *L'Agnese va a morire* (1949).

Vittorini, Elio (1908-66). Novelist and influential cultural operator; moved from youthful 'left' Fascism to Marxism; founded innovative postwar journals (*Politecnico*, 1945-47; *Il menabò*, 1959-67) and book series for Einaudi; wrote experimental, symbolist/realist novels (e.g. *Conversazione in Sicilia*, 1941).

Volponi, Paolo (1924-94). Novelist, as well as poet and critic; worked for Olivetti; interested in the world of industry, the factory and modern work (*Memoriale*, 1962; *Le mosche del capitale*, 1989).

Zanzotto, Andrea (1921-). Major poet and critic; his work is characterised by sophisticated linguistic and formal experimentation, as well as subtle humour and elegance; associated with Veneto region (Pieve di Soligo). Collections include *Dietro il paesaggio* (1951), *La beltà* (1968), *Il Galateo in bosco* (1978).

Zavattini, Cesare (1902-89). Screenwriter/director, novelist, essayist, journalist; central theorist and screenwriter of Neo-Realist cinema; he also wrote comic and satirical material in several arenas.

Index

Index